Palaces of Rome

Fabio Benzi
Caroline Vincenti Montanaro

Palaces of Rome

Photography
Roberto Schezen

RIZZOLI
NEW YORK

Photo credits:
pp. 6, 20, 71: Araldo De Luca, Rome
p. 108: Archivio Fotografico Musei Capitolini, Rome
pp. 23, 96, 151, 214, 216, 284, 289, 297: Archivio Scala, Florence
pp. 52, 112, 146, 160, 180, 282: Istituto Nazionale per la Grafica, Rome
pp. 8–29, 44, 124, 146, 208, 230, 242: Michele Crosera, Venice
p. 40: Musei Vaticani, photo Pietro Zigrossi, Rome

First published in the United States of America in 1997 by
Rizzoli International Publications, Inc.
300 Park Avenue South, New York, NY 10010

First published in Italy in 1997 by
Arsenale Editrice srl
San Polo 1789
I-30125 Venezia

ISBN 0-8478-2056-4
LC 97-68125

Translated from the Italian by Jay Hyams

Printed by EBS-Editoriale Bortolazzi-Stei, Verona

Printed in Italy

Table of Contents

Palaces and Villas in Rome from the Renaissance to the Late Baroque

Fabio Benzi

The palace and the villa are architectural types, but both are also physical expressions of historical ideas. Behind both of them stands the city of Rome. The very word *palace* is derived from the Latin form of Palatine, the hill in Rome where the emperors' stately residences were built; and the villas of the Renaissance were designed in imitation of those of imperial Rome, so much so that they were often built on the site of ancient examples. Even more important, however, is the fact that from the period of the Renaissance through the eighteenth century, Rome played a vital role in the history of how the palace and the villa evolved as concepts and as solid realities. It was in Rome that the experimentation took place, just as it was in Rome that the most outstanding examples, the buildings that can be considered emblematic of each type, were built and studied. In the same way that the architecture of Rome in the sixteenth and seventeenth centuries came to serve as the primary example for the development of the architectural language throughout Europe, the palace and the villa as architectural types led to highly original creations in Rome that then went on to inspire imitations far beyond the walls of that city.

A brief introduction to the subject cannot go into great detail, nor is there room here to mention each of the buildings that is today considered important to the evolution in architectural thought that eventually led to the complex themes expressed by palaces and villas. The same is true of the choice of the palaces and villas that are presented in this book: the selection is by no means exhaustive and does not include all of the major examples, for it seemed wiser, given the dense fabric of buildings in the city, to include a few less famous, less well-visited examples. It is hoped that this wider coverage will offer the reader a better sense of the enormous wealth of buildings still preserved within the Aurelian walls.

Palaces and villas are distinct types of structures. They differ both in how they are used and in their architectural characteristics. Because of these differences, it might seem odd to deal with both types in a single book. The reasons for doing so are directly related to the urban realities of Rome from the fifteenth to the eighteenth centuries.

Rome experienced a rebirth, both morally and architecturally, with the return to the city of the popes at the end of the so-called Babylonian captivity (1309–78), during which the popes had been French and had lived at Avignon. The years of the papal absence were part of centuries of large-scale decline and deterioration in

The piazza of the Campidoglio was designed by Michelangelo, who had to unify the preexisting and heterogeneous structures. The work continued long after his death, but the piazza, together with the three palaces and the staircase, reflects his plans faithfully.

the city. The revival began slowly but soon reached considerable proportions. It can be said to have had its true beginning in 1417 with the installation of Oddone Colonna on the papal throne as Martin V (1417–31). As a member of one of the leading families, he was able to command a high level of political control in the city, where rival factions had long been exploiting the power vacuum.

When Martin V began his reign the great city was really more of a town, its inhabitants crowded into dilapidated structures located almost entirely in the bend of the Tiber River between the Campidoglio and the Castel Sant'Angelo Bridge. Most of the area enclosed within the ancient walls of imperial Rome was uninhabited and had become rolling fields strewn with the ruins of collapsed buildings, broad open spaces used as pasture. Some of these fields came to be called *vigna*, a word that means "vineyard" but was applied to the cultivated land around villas, a usage that continued into the eighteenth century. Standing out above the other buildings were the city's great churches, but these holy structures stood alone, each surrounded by a few houses, almost creating a separate village.

Many of Europe's cities had similar unused areas during this period—a variety of calamities, in particular plagues, had drastically diminished local populations—but the situation in Rome was striking. The custom arose in the fifteenth century of using these open areas to create urban gardens, most of which were furnished with one or more pavilions, most often small structures but sometimes quite large ones, in which the free hours of the day could be spent in idle leisure. Over the centuries, as the city grew and the built-up area extended up to the ancient walls and even went beyond them, these open spaces disappeared, and many of the gardens became enclosed within the urban fabric; the pavilions that survived were then transformed into true palaces.

The architectural types called villas and palaces are thus related, or at least closely tied, at a certain level, for they had in common certain forms and functions and were created as evocations of the same version of beauty. There is, for example, the Quirinal, which came into being as a summer residence for the popes and was later transformed into a palace; there is the nearby Palazzo Barberini, which was originally conceived as an emulation of the Renaissance villa, surrounded by a garden and located on a far edge of the city's expansion, but which certainly meets the criteria of a "palace," although it is quite innovative for that genre. The great availability of land within the city of Rome combined with the presence of a well-to-do clientele eager for a context in which to pursue aesthetic and social pleasures created the perfect situation for architectural experimentation. Buildings were built to serve official functions; others were intended as elegant residences. The architects in Rome were easily able to compare these types, and not just because the buildings were physically close together but also because they were close in architectural concept. This ongoing comparison, and the fact that the architects active in Rome included some of the greatest of their period, enriched the architecture of the city with innovative ideas that influenced design all across Europe.

The Origins of the Roman Palace in the Age of Humanism

During the early years of the fifteenth century, Rome found itself in an extremely precarious situation. Despite various half-hearted efforts to kindle "rebirths" in the twelfth and thirteenth centuries, the city had known centuries of almost absolute neglect. The inhabited areas of the city were run-down and impoverished, and the immense expanses in which the great public buildings and temples of imperial Rome had once stood were in a state of ruin. The remains of the ancient buildings and the random array of ramshackle structures built on top of or alongside them gave Rome the landscape typical of a medieval city. Narrow, tortuous streets wound around open fields heaped with ancient rubble or went past buildings constructed in no particular style and in shapes meant to adapt to the shapes of previous structures, such as the palaces and piazzas with curvilinear shapes atop theaters or amphitheaters. The few monumental buildings still in use, such as the Pantheon, were surrounded by grim huts that only further insulted their past grandeur. During the more prosperous periods of the Middle Ages, some of the streets had been given porticoes using slabs of marble stripped from the columns of temples and public buildings (some of these chunks of marble are still visible in the walls of many palaces within the bend of the Tiber). But these porticoes had later been filled in with rubble and crude temporary structures, becoming impassable and useful only as receptacles for garbage. In the second half of the fifteenth century, Bartolomeo Platina, Martin V's biographer, described Rome as it was at the beginning of that pope's reign: "The Rome he found was a Rome crumbling and collapsing, a city in such a state of devastation that it could hardly have been considered fit for human habitation: whole rows of houses abandoned by their tenants; many churches fallen to the ground; streets deserted and

ABOVE: Designed during the pontificate of Paolo II (c. 1467–70), this house was constructed as many other Roman buildings during the first half of the century. It was built on preexisting foundations without a symmetrical or coordinated architectural plan.

BELOW: Built by Paolo II, Palazzo Venezia is the first large palace of the Renaissance. Showing ties with tradition, the splendor of the rooms and of the decorative and architectural elements is fundamental for the evolution of the Roman Renaissance.

buried under heaps of refuse; traces of plague and famine everywhere. It was a city thoroughly worn out by poverty."

Given this dire situation, it is not surprising that the efforts of the popes to rebuild the city, beginning with the works under Martin V, were first directed at restoring the buildings that were in a state of collapse, in particular the principal churches, and at improving the overall urban condition. In fact, the popes at first followed no particular building policy, and even in terms of private homes no important steps were taken toward developing specific building types until the pontificate of Nicholas V (1447–55). The great architects of the early Renaissance, such as Filippo Brunelleschi (1377–1446) and Leon Battista Alberti (1404–1472), visited Rome to study the remains of the city's ancient buildings, and those structures inspired their own work. But their buildings were not in Rome; in fact, no important buildings were constructed in the city itself until the middle of the century. Thus the Colosseum inspired Alberti in his creation of Palazzo Rucellai in Florence, and Brunelleschi got the basic idea behind his Palazzo Pitti, the prototype of the Renaissance palace in Florence, from the rusticated walls of the forum of Nerva. During this period Rome saw the building of only much simpler types, houses with plaster walls given graffitowork decoration and cross-mullioned, or Guelf, windows. In Florence, most of the patrons for new buildings were members of the nouveau-riche middle class, people with money to spend and an eagerness to show off their newfound status; this situation led to the development of expressions of dignified wealth, adding new forms to the already mixed fabric of the city, forms of geometric and symbolic purity. In Rome, on the other hand, most of the clients were members of the high clergy—men not eager for the outward display of riches—so the Roman palace came into being in a situation in which less importance was given to the external expression of the facade (which in many cases had to include a tower, symbol of a cardinal's dignity); instead, more attention was given to the comfortable and sumptuous arrangement of the interior rooms.

Of course, the exterior of a palace must have some correspondence, at least in shape, to its interior arrangement and to its side; usually the ground plan does not mask any asymmetries. Thus fifteenth-century Roman palaces always have a nongeometric shape, but in each case the shape fits the building's interior rooms or its location. In Rome, old buildings were incorporated into new ones rather than being razed; indeed, there was no indication of a "regularizing" norm being applied to the urban fabric,

PALAZZO RIARIO ALTEMPS,
ROOM OF THE PIATTAIA

This fresco is one of the rare examples of decoration in a fifteenth-century Roman palace.

This original subject was probably developed by Pedro Berruguete during his stay in Rome around 1480–81.

as was the case in Florence, where the perfect cube of Palazzo Strozzi became a sort of template, an exceptional example to be followed by others. Even the most elaborate palace of fifteenth-century Rome, the Cancelleria, whose dressing in travertine marble and moldings of carved marble can be taken as preludes to sixteenth-century opulence, has a strangely irregular layout that could easily have been made into a regular geometric shape. And the windows in the facade of the city's other great palace of that period, the Palazzo Venezia, built for Cardinal Pietro Barbo, later elected pope as Paul II (1464–71), follow an irregular order, a result of their being made to serve the needs of the interior rooms. The architects of Rome seem to have looked on the notion of trying to apply some sort of abstract, external regularity to palaces as something foreign or at least inappropriate, and instead they based their designs on the opulence of interior decorations and on the humanistic citations made by antiquarian elements, present in the sculptural parts of buildings, and in the classical lexicon expressed by other individual elements.

Only the dimmest traces—for the most part in documents, not stone—remain of the Roman palaces that were built during the first half of the fifteenth century, but they probably differed very little from the late medieval model, except for the adoption of certain "modern" elements, such as the cross-mullioned window. This is still evident in the Mattei family palazzetto in the Piazza in Piscinula, built during the pontificate of Paul II. The very disappearance of most of these "spontaneous" constructions testifies to their poor quality in terms of design (most were made to incorporate preexisting structures), to the poor quality of the building materials used, and to their dreary sameness. For these reasons, they were replaced by more modern and sumptuous palaces, palaces more suitable to the expression of the dignity and wealth of Rome during the Renaissance and the baroque.

Although their interiors have been greatly reworked, the Vatican Palace of the period of Pope Nicholas V, built between 1447 and 1454, and the Palazzo Capranica, completed around 1451, are the best remaining examples of early residential palaces. Nicholas V's palace was part of a grandiose scheme of urban renewal in Rome that was centered on the area of the Vatican and probably involved at least the advice of Leon Battista Alberti. Very little of this plan was actually carried out, but the palace remains as practically the first monumental residential building in fifteenth-century Rome. The palace's exterior is very simple; it is horizontal in shape, composed of three floors standing on a slop-

ing pedestal, and it ends at the top in a crenellated cornice; the large windows are cross-mullioned, and the layout is composed basically of two perpendicular wings. The facade was of plaster decorated with graffitowork and faux rustications, and the effect combined elements of both fortress and palace, as did the later, more famous Palazzo Venezia. All the luxury was reserved for the sumptuous decoration of the interior rooms, two of which were frescoed by Fra Angelico (only the splendid chapel of Nicholas V remains today). Bernardo Rossellino (c. 1407–1469), the "palace engineer" of Nicholas V from 1451 to 1453, must have been responsible for the design, but the great changes that have been made to the building over the course of centuries make it difficult to get more than a general sense of the original design. Even so, a period source (Rucellai) records attached "gardens, large and small, with a pond and water fountain and rabbit hutch," which calls attention once again to how, from its earliest origins, the Roman palace shared many characteristics with the "villa." For its part, Palazzo Capranica confirms the established type of the cardinal's palace: a rectangular block of three floors (of which the second is the *nobile*, meaning its rooms are larger than those on the other floors) with a facade marked off irregularly with cross-mullioned windows, and to one side a tower announcing the rank of the palace's owner.

The plaster used to cover the surfaces of fifteenth-century Roman palaces was obviously less expensive than the rusticated stone employed so often in Florence, but the plaster was often embellished with graffitowork decoration that evolved from the simple presentation of faux rustication into far more complex types using moldings, plant motifs, candelabra, frames, and figures, finally leading in the sixteenth century to the magnificent painted facades with historical and allegorical scenes done by the school of Raphael (most of all by Polidoro da Caravaggio), of which Palazzo Massimo and Palazzo Ricci are magnificent examples.

Palazzo Venezia was the first great Roman palace in the modern, Renaissance sense, but its facade is marked by the same sense of simplicity that we have been discussing: with crenellations at top, and plastered walls, cross-mullioned windows, and the usual cardinal's tower. However, the architect who designed it, Francesco del Borgo (d. 1468), made it into a masterpiece of the Renaissance spirit.

Papal functionary, book illuminator, and architect, Francesco was given humanistic training in antiquarian and literary subjects, not in architecture in the usual sense, so his education resembled

that of Leon Battista Alberti, whom he certainly knew. In fact, the conception of the more monumental elements of the palace seem based on ideas from Alberti. For example, there is the magnificent atrium with a barrel vault and coffered ceiling (in Book IX of his architectural treatise *De re aedificatoria*, the section dedicated to palaces, Alberti prescribed a "a luminous, broad vestibule"); there are also the unfinished courtyard, in an arrangement that recalls the not distant arcades of the Colosseum, the portico with two orders of the incorporated basilica of San Marco, the attached garden, and the vast halls with their coffered ceilings. Even the air of "severity" of the exterior echoes Alberti's opinions ("in their decoration, city homes must have an air of severity far greater than that of villas"), although the crenellations do not. Alberti advised against using crenellations for city palaces, but they were in keeping with Roman usage. The events in the palace's history illuminate the irregularities of its building. Pietro Barbo was made cardinal of the Church of San Marco in 1451; between 1454 and 1455 he decided to rebuild the cardinal's palace at the side of the church, and this work was completed shortly before his election as Pope Paul II in 1464. This first palace included the wing today facing Piazza Venezia, up to but excluding the main door; it was lower and did not have a courtyard. After Barbo's election as pope he decided to transform it into a grandiose residence, and the work began in 1468. By the time of his death in 1471 work on this new palace had progressed up to the main door on Via del Plebiscito, and it continued for another twenty years.

With the death of Paul II, Sixtus IV (1471–84) came to the throne. Today considered the greatest pope of the fifteenth century, he was the pope most responsible for bringing Rome into the true spirit of the Renaissance. His pontificate was a period of enormous building in Rome, but most of these efforts were dedicated to public buildings and churches—the Sistine Chapel, for example, which is named for him. No residential buildings of particular importance were built during his rule, but the taste for marble decorations inspired by antiquity increased enormously, as is clear in the reworking of the internal rooms of the cardinal's

palace of SS Apostoli by Baccio Pontelli (1450–1494), Sixtus IV's favorite architect. Baccio had been born into a family of Florentine carpenters and had served as palace architect at the Urbino court, where he had executed intarsia for the wooden *studiolo* made for Duke Federigo da Montefeltro. In Rome, he became a major disseminator of ideas from Tuscany and humanist Urbino. An extraordinary fresco with illusionistic decoration was recently uncovered in Palazzo Riario (today Palazzo Altemps). Attributed to the hand of a foreign painter (this author believes the most likely candidate to be the Spaniard Pedro Berruguete, active, like Pontelli, at the Urbino court), it gives an idea of the decorative opulence of Roman palaces, and in that sense it also confirms the Roman vision, completely the opposite of that of Florence, where interiors were far simpler and exteriors were made with expensive marble finishings.

The most important palace of the fifteenth century, the project that brought together all the energy of Sixtus and projected it toward the new century, was the Cancelleria, built between 1483–84 and 1495 for Cardinal Raffaele Riario, Sixtus IV's nephew. The architect who designed it was almost certainly Baccio Pontelli, and with its design he radically altered the image of the noble residence in Rome. The broad facade incorporates the church of San Lorenzo in Damaso, almost transforming it into the palace's chapel, and the square block of the building is marked off by four towers (the usual cardinal symbols), transformed here into wings of the same height as the facade, that define the enormous expanse of the surface covered in lightly rusticated travertine marble. With this palace Pontelli introduced a new, highly modern style to Rome, taking the style that had made Urbino's Ducal Palace one of the reference points of the late fifteenth-century Renaissance and giving it a solemn, antiquarian, typically Roman appearance. The facade has three orders, the top two marked off by paired pilasters in a symmetrical, regular rhythm alternating with highly refined marble windows carved with antiquarian motifs, interpreting in a highly original and evocative manner the attic of the Colosseum and giving a revolutionary,

classical version of the Palazzo Rucellai by Alberti. The court-yard parts with the model established by Luciano Laurana in the Ducal Palace at Urbino, and is rendered with such a light, harmonious classicism that in the past it was regularly attributed to Donato Bramante. Sumptuous "antique-style" coffered ceilings completed the work, of which Pontelli made several studies that can be seen in the famous *Codex Escurialensis*, a work almost entirely by his hand.

Urban and Suburban Gardens: The Antiquarian Origins of the Roman Villa

Because of the large amount of open space available in the city, Rome began the fifteenth century by enriching itself with gardens, or *vigne*, furnished with pavilions for relaxation and entertainment. Most of these were located within the walls of the city, but in the more isolated and rustic areas.

These predecessors of the elaborate villas of the sixteenth century were themselves modest affairs, smaller and much plainer than any palace. Few examples of these early constructions survive today. The rambling gardens that once surrounded them have also long since disappeared beneath the urban sprawl of concrete. Even so, the history of the taste that led to their creation and their importance as early examples of an architectural genre can be reconstructed from period documents and chronicles, as seen in David R. Coffin's book *The Villa in the Life of Renaissance Rome*. The design of the gardens, as well as the inspiration for them, came from ancient sources that mention vast urban gardens spread with statues and fountains (the so-called *horti*, such as the celebrated gardens of Sallus and Maecenas). The nature of the city of Rome, with classical ruins located nearly everywhere, offered appropriate settings for the antiquarian taste of the humanists, and such areas could be further embellished with collections of ancient inscriptions and statues, objects that could then be used for meditation or become the subjects of erudite studies of scholars and connoisseurs of the antique. The

simpler casinos with their porticoes might be decorated with graffitowork on plaster, while the more elaborate examples, such as the later Villa Belvedere built (1485–87) under Pope Innocent VIII (1484–92) at the northern end of the Vatican hill, had frescoes of landscapes.

Most of these structures followed a rustic, irregular style of which the casino of Cardinal Bessarion near the walls of Rome on the Appian Way (c. 1460) can be taken as emblematic. This basic type remained substantially unchanged until early in the sixteenth century, but the more "noble" history of the Roman garden includes at least three important buildings. The first of these is the Palazzetto Venezia, a unique structure in its genre. It was basically a hanging garden surrounded by a portico. It was an external structure, but it was connected to Palazzo Venezia through a passage at one corner. Thus it does not fit within either the logic of the villa or that of the type of the palace garden, but is simply a caprice of Pope Paul II, who had it made between 1466 and 1468. Composed of an order of arches resting on octagonal piers, immediately followed by a second order on columns, the portico was surrounded by a wall with windows that gave directly on the outside.

The second important example is the so-called Palazzina of Cardinal Giuliano Della Rovere, which stood adjacent to SS Apostoli and was built in the years 1483 to 1485. Today it is mostly destroyed; remnants are incorporated in the Palazzo Colonna, but these remains are now obscured by later work. The Palazzina was built by the nephew of Sixtus IV, the future Pope Julius II, as a porticoed U-shaped loggia constructed in the middle of a large garden; the loggia was open on the ground floor and closed on the upper floor. It can be considered the direct predecessor of the Farnesia by Baldassare Peruzzi, considered the primary model of the Renaissance villa. Until recently, this derivation was not understood since the Palazzina was relatively unknown. On the other hand, the sumptuous fresco decorations of the loggia by Bernardino Pinturicchio (1488–91), the original opulence of the upper rooms, and most of all the porticoed structure recall with precision

the later interpretation of the frescoed loggias by Raphael, the luxury and the modern Renaissance conception of the villa of Agostino Chigi. Designed by Baccio Pontelli, who introduced the mature lexicon of the Renaissance to Roman architecture, the palazzina was surrounded by a garden in which the cardinal installed his collection of statues and bas-reliefs, first among these the *Apollo Belvedere*, originally found on one of his estates and today in the Vatican.

The third of these important structures is the loggia of the Belvedere in the Vatican, built between 1485 and 1487 for Pope Innocent VIII on the top of the Vatican hill and designed to exploit its panoramic view. Immersed in the greenery of a garden, this structure was dedicated to the liberal arts, which were presented on its walls alongside naturalistic landscapes and busts of prophets. The building included a chapel frescoed by Mantegna that was demolished when the villa was made part of the Museo Pio-Clementino at the end of the eighteenth century. The loggia included a small number of rooms arranged around a portico, built with arches, that serves as the fulcrum of the building. But the building has a slightly Gothic tone, evident in its shape and in the crenellations along the roofline, that makes it an evocative but by no means innovative example of the villa. Despite its irregular shape, which hints at the U-form inaugurated by Pontelli in the Palazzina, the opening toward the landscape is less broadly "Renaissance" (the raised loggia does not offer direct access to the garden), just as the conservative, somewhat "calligraphic" architecture recalls the works of Jacopo da Pietrasanta. A stonemason and architect, he is recorded as working on the loggia, but, unlike Pontelli, he made no reference to the new world about to appear with the new century.

The Renaissance Palace: Origins and Development of the Princely Home

The most brilliant period of Roman architecture began at the close of the fifteenth century (c. 1499) with the arrival in the city of Donato Bramante (c. 1444–1514). Born near Urbino and trained as a painter, Bramante is considered the founder of Roman High Renaissance architecture. His idea of reviving the grandeur and monumentality of ancient architecture by expressing it in modern buildings led to the fullest development of Renaissance architectural thought, and as such it prevailed not only in the architecture of Rome but in that of much of Europe well into the sixteenth century.

Although only a single palace (today destroyed) can be attributed without doubt to Bramante, he is known to have studied the form and infused it with new ideas. He preferred designing churches and other types of monumental architecture, but he also made numerous plans and designs for palaces that were either never built or on which he himself did not finish the work. He made designs for Vatican palaces (designs that are mentioned in documents but lost today), and he made designs for the Palazzo dei Tribunali on the Via Giulia (never finished and today practically destroyed) and for the loggias of the Vatican palaces in the courtyard of San Damaso (finished by Raphael).

The Palazzetto Caprini (built c. 1510 and also known as the House of Raphael, who bought it in 1517) is of great significance in the history of palace design, but is known today only from old engravings. It established a new type of facade using only two stories and giving each a different treatment. The orders on the two floors are clearly separated by an entablature. The lower floor

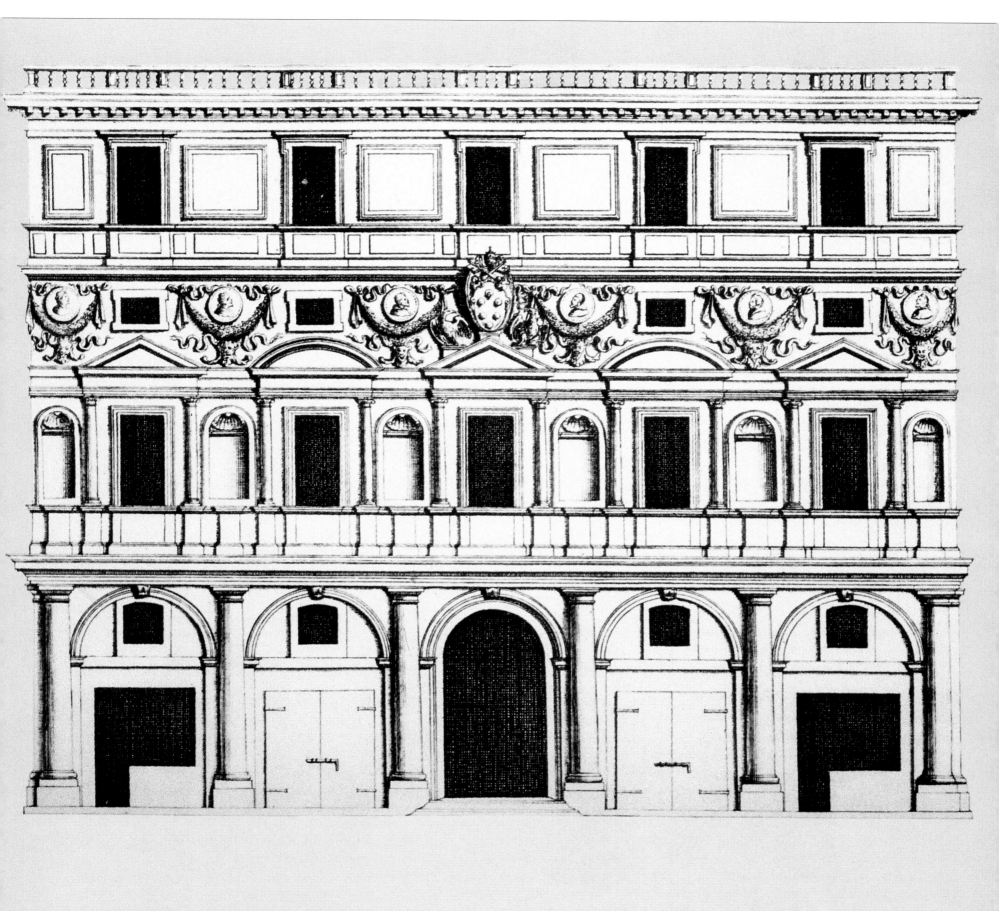

is a five-bay arcade with rough rustication; the upper *piano nobile* is far more elegant with pairs of Doric three-quarter columns, pedimented windows, balconies with balustrades, and pedestals that align with the thick piers of the arcade below.

Elements of this type, which can be seen as a means of translating classical, antiquarian notions in modern, plastic terms, were later used by Raphael in several of his buildings (such as Palazzo Jacopo da Brescia, c. 1512–16, and Palazzo Alberini, c. 1518). The form achieved even more success outside Rome, particularly in Venice where Jacopo Sansovino (1486–1570) experimented with it. The form of this style that came to predominate in Rome did indeed take its start with Bramante's idea but employed a simplified form, making it more versatile, almost modular. This is the version that was used so skillfully by Antonio da Sangallo the Younger, who first experimented with it in the little Palazzo Baldassini (1521–22) and then used it in his masterpiece, the Farnese Palace, the most beautiful palace of the Italian Renaissance. Sangallo used classical cornices to distinguish between the floors and employed rustication only to reinforce the corners. In this way he emphasized the sculptural, geometric mass of the building. The *piano nobile* is not marked off by rows of columns or pilasters; instead, the classical orders are used only in the window surrounds, their shape derived from the majestic niches in the Pantheon, but also comparable to more schematic cornices, such as those in Palazzo Baldassini. Thus was established a truly elegant model, one that was easy to replicate, easy to reproduce in variations. This model came to dominate Roman—

and European—architecture until the arrival of Bernini, and survived at least in terms of its basic outlines, all the way to the nineteenth century. The atrium became a space modeled on Roman single-cell temples (Palazzo Baldassini) or on ancient basilicas (Palazzo Farnese), both styles imbued with ancient nobility. The use of columns in the courtyard is abandoned completely, replaced by arcades supported by piers decorated with pilaster strips, on the model of the Vatican loggia by Bramante. Put briefly, Antonio da Sangallo took the classical language that Bramante and Raphael had established and defined—but with highly elegant accents and in a meticulously cultivated form—and made it more fluent and articulate, thus making a major contribution to its universal appeal.

Raphael himself was affected by these events and echoed them in his designs for Florence's Palazzo Pandolfini and Rome's Palazzo Branconio dell'Aquila. In particular, he limited the use of rustication to the main door and the corners of the building, and he stopped using architectural orders on facades. Even so, a refined antiquarianism remained alive in him that is reflected in the windows with three-quarter columns, pedestals, and balustrades with newels and the "antique-style" niches and stuccoes, all decorative and structural details that testify to an inventive genius who fitted architecture to his language rather than fitting his language to architecture, as did Sangallo.

Until the middle of the century, architects in Rome used the models created by Bramante and Sangallo to create a broad variety of imaginative and eclectic palaces. These structures were often imbued with an incomparable formal elegance, for they re-

FEDERICO ZUCCARI, PALAZZETTO ZUCCARI ON VIA GREGORIANA

In this ultimate expression of the architectural mannerism of Rome, Zuccari's "whim" combines urban and grotesque elements reserved for gardens of villas.

flect the princely and luxurious lives led by their owners, who surrounded themselves with collections of statues and paintings and had their rooms frescoed with scenes that were usually secular and quite often purely hedonistic. The palace was adapted to serve the sumptuous life of the new princes of the church and the members of their courts, many of whom still sought to ignore the bans and rules of the growing Reformation movement and the difficult international political situation in general—and this despite the upheaval of the sack of the city in 1527.

The structures built in this period include works by Baldassare Peruzzi, whose Palazzo Massimo alle Colonne (1532–36) is a decidedly original version of a manneristic palace. With its porticoed facade and decorations of an admirable antiquarian eclecticism, it presents a version of the palace in which the restraint of Raphael is being steadily replaced by the anxious *horror vacui* of mannerism. Giulio Romano designed the Palazzo Stati Maccarani (c. 1521; today Palazzo Di Brazzà), which emphasizes and "giganticizes" the subtle measurements of Raphael. The small Palazzetto Leroy by Antonio da Sangallo (c. 1523) is covered by so many experiments in materials and forms—loggias, Serilan motifs, pediments, different sizes of rustication, carved cornices—that it presents a vaguely unsettling catalog of classical details. And Palazzo Spada, made during the middle of the century, follows the example of Raphael's Palazzo Branconio dell'Aquila and is covered with stuccoes and paintings by Mazzoni, making it a refined example of the "international" mannerist style.

A drive toward greater simplicity, at least in terms of external elements, began taking the upper hand around the 1540s. This led to the triumph of the Sangallo model and was more in keeping with the mood being generated by the forces of the Counter Reformation. Palazzo Sacchetti (c. 1543, begun by Antonio da Sangallo) looks like a fortress; Palazzo Massimo Lancellotti, a work by Pirro Ligorio (c. 1513–1583), one of the most imaginative and eclectic mannerist architects, is held tight within bare and deliberately ascetic measurements. Following a model by Sangallo, it is decorated only by continuous stucco rustication. Annibale Lippi's Palazzo Caetani repeats the simplicity of this same design.

It seems unlikely that Michelangelo could have successfully adapted his genius to fit this trend, but then he dealt with the subject of the residential palace only once, in his work completing Palazzo Farnese. He built the magnificent, powerful cornice, centralized the facade, and designed the main window with marble columns in its surrounds and over it the dramatic Farnese coat of arms. By doing so he radically reworked Sangallo's refined sobriety and "orderliness." Michelangelo did nothing to alter the general layout of the palace's courtyard, but he gave it windows with capricious surrounds decorated with bucranes and garlands. It was in the Palazzo dei Conservatori in the Campidoglio that Michelangelo inaugurated a new type, that of the "giant" order: the two floors are joined by grandiose pilaster strips (a motif that became widespread in the palaces of European nobility because of the monumental spirit they inspire). He articulated the masses of the floors in a way that was anything but "minimalist"—strongly chiaroscuro, almost in relief—and he placed statues along the top as though to emphasize the classical inspiration, also highly evident in the use of sculptural details as structural elements.

Michelangelo's innovations were not immediately imitated in the design of Roman palaces; the true heirs to his creativity were to appear only in the following century, beginning with the great architects of the baroque. Instead, the leading architects of the second half of the sixteenth century—most of all Domenico

Fontana, Giacomo della Porta, Ottaviano Mascherino, and Martino Longhi—dedicated themselves to building evocative variations on the established Sangallo theme. The ostentatious display applied to exteriors during the first half of the century was redirected inward and applied instead to the interior rooms. Indeed, decorations come to occupy more and more of the interior space, with fresco cycles, stuccowork, elaborate wooden coffered ceilings, and sumptuous furnishings filling the available space; at the same time, the exteriors pay homage to the principles of the Counter Reformation by displaying only a sober *dignitas*, their simple monumentality stripped of all decorative exuberance.

The Renaissance Villa as a Place for Pleasure and Erudite Meditation

The desire to lead a cultured and refined life, with moments of relaxation passed in pleasant contact with nature or in humanistic studies, reached its peak at the beginning of the sixteenth century. It was during these years that the original fifteenth-century *vigna*, with its rustic character and antiquarian ornaments, evolved into a luxurious house—but by no means a home to be inhabited. It was instead a place for entertainment, a setting whose opulent decorations, collections of antiquities, and frescoes by noted artists would, taken together, constitute an "object" of supreme originality.

Baldassare Peruzzi took the example of the Palazzina of Giuliano Della Rovere near SS Apostoli designed by Pontelli and codified its design and spirit to create a type of building. Then, between 1507 and 1511, he applied that type to the villa he built for the banker Agostino Chigi, which was later owned by the Farnese family and thus known as the Farnesina. In this villa, the U-shaped layout becomes a means for opening on to and embracing nature, a sense that is heightened by the ground-floor loggia, which creates a continuous interchange between the villa's interior and exterior. The external surfaces of the villa are enclosed within the standard classical orders, but with a delicate harmony; the decoration was done by Raphael, Peruzzi himself, and other artists, including Sebastiano del Piombo and Sodoma, with scenes that are a sort of apologia to the pagan world of antiquity. The garden along the Tiber looks out onto the ruins of ancient Rome and the buildings of the modern city.

During this early period of the Renaissance, and until the sack of 1527, the motifs of antiquity provided inspiration for a civilization that felt it was on the way to regaining the heights of past imperial splendors. The desire to bring the ancient villa back to life in a modern style can be seen in the so-called Villa Madama, designed around 1518 by Raphael for Cardinal Giulio de' Medici, a cousin of Pope Leo X. In this design Raphael made use of information then coming to light from the excavation of ancient villas, together with ideas from Vitruvius. Many aspects of the new Roman villas reflect this urge to repeat ancient models, ranging from the wide barrel vaults with their coffered ceilings (based on those of ancient Roman baths) to the subjects of the decorations, making much use of grotesques and pagan scenes. Terraced and laid out following a geometric design, the villa's gardens are a harbinger of the design concepts of the Italian-style garden, an overly decorated garden in which nature is made to fit symmetrical forms following a markedly architectural and theatrical design, with geometric flowerbeds, straight pathways, stairways, ponds, fountains, and statues: a model that all of Europe would follow for centuries to come.

It was Raphael's favorite student, Giulio Romano, who made the mannerist masterpiece of Villa Lante on the Janiculum Hill,

built on the site of a villa owned by the Roman writer Martial (A.D. 40–104). Little more than a loggia, it opens out on the highest point of the hill so as to look straight down on the city. Elements from Bramante and motifs from Serlio lighten the building to the point that it seems to dematerialize against the sky.

The passion for studying and making use of motifs from the ancient past continued unabated following the sack of Rome in 1527, but not in exactly the same way. The "classical" came to lose more and more of its sharpness, its "true" character; antiquity, in a sense, came to be less directly experienced and was treated more as repertory, almost as though the awareness was prevailing that the glories of the past really were not repeatable, only collectible. Furthermore, following the process taking place in the design of palaces, luxury and opulence in villas were directed inward, toward the interior decoration of rooms and the secret pleasures of the inner garden, while the part of the villa facing the street was provided with a simpler, more subdued appearance. Thus the facade of Villa Giulia, designed by Giacomo da Vignola (1507–1573) for Pope Julius III in the 1550s, is simple and bare, with rustications its only decorations. Inside the villa are loggias

covered with frescoes by the Zuccaro brothers, a nymphaeum "all'antica" made by Ammanati in a visionary style of mannerism, and shrines and pavilions scattered across an immense park. The "pagan" splendors of the villa were criticized even by contemporaries of the pope, but the pleasures of villas continued to win out over the moral preachings of the Counter Reformation. Villa Medici, with its garden designed by Nanni di Baccio Bigio and his son Annibale Lippi in the 1560s, presents the city with a face of bare simplicity—in truth, its facade gives it the sense of being a fortress—but the other side, the side facing the garden, is something entirely different. The loggia is of impressive richness (made in the early 1580s by Lorenzetto following a style begun by Pirro Ligorio in the Casino of Pius IV), and the garden facade itself is inlaid with a profusion of ancient bas-reliefs, busts, and stuccoes. Pavilions with frescoes of naturalistic subjects are placed throughout the park, creating oases of unexpected refinement for every hour of the day and evoking the descriptions of the pavilions in the famous Roman *horti* (gardens).

It was around 1560 that Pirro Ligorio made the Casino of Pius IV, located within the Vatican gardens, which already housed

Ligorio built this small house in the Vatican Gardens between 1559 and 1562. It is elaborately antique in its conception, in which the mannerist vision takes hold of, yet twists, the pure rediscovery of antiquity in the Renaissance.

Carlo Maderno and Gian Lorenzo Bernini, Palazzo Barberini. Begun by Maderno according to a traditional plan, Bernini finished the palace with the large loggia in splayed perspective, fundamentally innovating the concept of the palatial facades, giving them a decidedly baroque impression.

the fifteenth-century Belvedere and the court designed by Bramante. Ligorio also added terraces and fountains that express the sum total of the Roman taste for things antiquarian, which by then was heading toward a kind of overdecorated mannerism, balanced between the idea of rules and that of transgression, between the serious study of the past and the pleasure to be taken in its interpretation. The *Horti Farnesiani* of Pope Paul III offer a slightly different side of this "contamination" of the ancient and the modern by presenting an evocative comparison between the true antiquities of the Palatine and the invented antiquities of pavilions, fountains, grottoes, statues, and Italian-style gardens. It is a picturesque comparison in which the example of antiquity comes to serve as background for the marvelous and playful arrangement of the luxurious garden, a site for earthly delights.

The Villa Peretti Montalto (demolished during construction of Rome's train station), designed after 1576 by Domenico Fontana for Cardinal Felice Peretti, later Sixtus V, is an example of the style of the Roman villa at the end of the sixteenth century. The Italian-style gardens grew larger, with more fountains and increasingly elaborate jets of water, and the secondary buildings grew larger too, and more theatrical, until they were large enough to serve as true summer residences.

The Baroque Palace

During the transitional period between the close of the sixteenth century and the opening of the mature baroque period in architecture at the end of the 1720s, architects of great professional stature were active in Rome, preparing the way for the epiphanies of the grandiose new style. Ottaviano Mascherino, Flaminio Ponzio, but most of all Carlo Maderno (nephew of Domenico Fontana) proved themselves inventive designers. Working within the late sixteenth-century vocabulary, they created spatial innovations and new decorative types that made way for the new style and that culminated in the revolutionary work of Bernini, Borromini, and Pietro da Cortona. In Palazzo Borghese, Flaminio Ponzio (succeeding Martino Longhi I) created illusionistic and theatrical flourishes that came to form part of the thematic repertory of the baroque. The far end of the monumental courtyard with its paired columns opens on the garden and the sky, thus breaking free of the enclosed spaces of the sixteenth century and inaugurating a new field of perspective in which luminosity and illusion are interwoven. In a similar way, the interior rooms are arranged in long series that run back toward the vanishing point, reflecting a highly original and expanded sense of monumentality. Maderno began Palazzo Barberini around 1625, leaving it unfinished at his death (1629), when it was completed by Bernini with the assistance of Borromini. It was conceived with an unusual form, resting on the U-shape typical of the urban villa (such as the Farnesina), reflecting its location on the periphery of the city and on the presence of the large surrounding garden. In forcing the building's layout to fit an "unsuitable" site, Maderno performed a typically baroque operation of blending, the kind of operation Bernini brought to a revolutionary level by making the great loggia open on the facade, bending inward surfaces outward in a way the sixteenth-century world would never have conceived.

Bernini brought many innovations to the design of palaces: emphasis on a palace's spatial reality, its theatrical presence within the fabric of a city, with facades that follow new layout types whose purpose is the representation of magnificent power. The stairway in Palazzo Barberini is supported by paired columns and ascends by way of concentric ramps that amplify the theme of the spiral stairway and transform its layout into a square figure in which light falls from above, creating multiple, changing perspectives. The facade of the Palazzo di Montecitorio, commissioned by the Ludovisi family and later by Pope Pamphili at the middle of

FRANCESO BORROMINI, ROOF-
TERRACE OF THE FALCONIERI PALACE

Utilizing "classical" elements,
Borromini gave a new sense
to architectural language: plas-
matic as sculpture, the space is
activated by the embossed and
chiaroscuroed trimming, in which
the decorative elements are
imbued with a new and vibrant
sense of structure.

OPPOSITE: PIETRO OF CORTONA,
PALAZZO BARBERINI, TRIUMPH OF
DIVINE PROVIDENCE

Painted between 1633 and 1639,
the ceiling is the most sumptuous
of the seventeenth century.

the century, combines multiple levels in oblique movement, suggesting an accentuated perspective flight and breaking the rectangular, flat scheme that was until then common. The rustications supporting the ground floor, which in turn supports the giant orders of the upper floors, include irregular illusionistic rocks in a nature–architecture mimesis typical of the baroque. The facade of the Palazzo Chigi-Odescalchi is also given perspective movement, with wings that bend back and a central section marked by a giant order that elaborates the Michelangelo model of the Capitoline palaces by raising it on a base composed of a ground floor, suggesting a theme further elaborated by later architects from Guarini to Juvarra to Fisher von Erlach.

Borromini designed highly sophisticated decorative details for palaces, complex and symbolic images whose capricious originality and aggressive manner of filling space awaken a sense of wonder. The windows and doorways he created for Palazzo Barberini reveal a restless force that curls back window surrounds and bizarre pediments, surprising forms with undulating rhythms that continue to spread in the numerous restorations of Roman palaces (Spada, Carpegna, Pamphili in Piazza Navona, Falconieri) for which he made the doorways, ceilings, windows, and room decorations. Although he made many designs for palaces, he never made an entire palace except for the Propaganda Fide (which was not a residential place) and the Spada family's palace

on Monte Giordano (destroyed). Nevertheless, the originality of his work had repercussions until well into the next century, with the evolution of the rococo and even the visionary neoclassicism of Piranesi.

Pietro da Cortona (1596–1669) made several scenic designs for palaces, but he built none. Even so, with the ceiling he made in Palazzo Barberini (1633–39) he made a decisive contribution to the decorative taste of baroque interiors. No more than a few years earlier, he had made frescoes in the gallery of the Palazzo Mattei that are still based on a scheme of Carracci-style *quadrature*; but in his work in Palazzo Barberini he performed a dramatic unleashing of the scene, which expands across the open sky, fulfilling the mature vision of the baroque. Thus the cycles of wall frescoes of fifteenth- and sixteenth-century palaces were replaced by frescoed vaults, leaving the walls of palaces open for the display of the collections of paintings that the great families were assembling and for the pieces of elegant furniture in the most bizarre baroque style. This change also reflects changes in methods of palace construction, for the wooden floors and coffered ceilings of the fifteenth and sixteenth century were being replaced by vast barrel vaults, giving baroque interiors a heightened sense of nobility and grandeur.

Other architects active in Rome alongside Borromini and Bernini contributed its seventeenth-century face. There was Camillo Arcucci, who presented original versions of the basic models in Palazzo Gottifredi-Grazioli and, most of all, in the facade of Palazzo Pio dei Carpi at the middle of the century. Martino Longhi II's masterpiece was the stairway he made in Palazzo Ruspoli, a work on the border between mannerist caprice and baroque fancy. Giovanni Antonio de Rossi was one of the most talented palace architects of the period: from the Altieri, in which the various spaces are all based on courtyards and stairways that are not ingenious but that present efficient drama, up to his masterpiece, Palazzo d'Aste Bonaparte on Piazza Venezia, modulated by curvilinear, plastic areas with unusual, curving and arching pediments, and showing an effect of elegant, decorative dash. And Girolamo and Carlo Rainaldi made the design for Palazzo Pamphili in Piazza Navona.

The construction explosion began ebbing at the end of the century, with most of the money spent going to churches. The deaths of the great masters of the baroque led to a period of stasis in ideas: instead of new buildings, the city saw reworkings or ele-

gant reproductions of already affirmed models. The architects most active in this were Carlo Rainaldi (Palazzo Mancini in the Via del Corso, c. 1662, the nymphaeum of the Borghese Palace, 1672–73), Mattia de Rossi, Carlo Fontana (the highly original door for the Palazzo Massimi, 1695, and the completion of the Bernini facade of Palazzo Montecitorio, with the crowning of the central part and the classical main door, 1694–97).

The Baroque Villa: Elegance and Luxury

The decorative and dramatic grandeur that Domenico Fontana presented in the Villa Peretti found its resounding continuation in the seventeenth century. Villas evolved from places for private meditation or learned assemblies to sumptuous settings in which illusionistic perspective is conveyed by infinite metamorphic variations of plants, sprays of water, statues, and pavilions.

The beginning of this vogue based on luxury and on the most refined and awesome grandeur is marked by the works commissioned by Scipione Borghese, Pope Paul V's strong-willed and megalomaniacal nephew. Giovanni Vasanzio was the versatile interpreter, with the occasional collaboration of Flaminio Ponzio and Carlo Maderno, of this taste for elegance that marks the passage from mannerism to the baroque. Beginning with the examples of Pirro Ligorio and Lorenzetto, Vasanzio made the opulent casino of Villa Borghese, reworking designs by Ponzio (c. 1609) and using decorative stucco frames to attach 144 bas-reliefs, 70 busts, and 43 ancient statues to the facade; Girolamo Rainaldi made the Uccelliera and the Green Theater, buildings of unreal spaciousness, encircled by an immense park. Vasanzio also enriched the Vatican gardens with bizarre, dreamy fountains (Fontana dell'Aquila, 1614, and della Galera, 1620) and worked on Palazzo Pallavicini Rospigliosi and on the pavilions in the park (Casino dell'Aurora).

Villa Borghese, conceived as a showcase to display the fabulous collection of paintings and statues amassed by Scipione Borghese, set an example that was followed by other prosperous Roman families. Many of these families acquired immense parks in which geometric Italian-style gardens alternated with rambling woodlands, areas spread with fountains and lakes and inhabited by rare birds and animals. Within their precincts were luxurious, evocative buildings decorated by the leading artists of the day. These parks were always within or quite nearby the walls of the city, but they were no longer the intimate settings they had been

in the sixteenth century and were instead hyperbolic demonstrations of power and wealth. In 1622, Cardinal Ludovico Ludovisi began work on an enormous villa that came to incorporate five buildings. For its decoration, he called on Guercino (1591–1666), who made a famous fresco in the Casino dell'Aurora, the only extant part of the villa. Domenichino (1581–1641) designed part of the garden, in which the famous collection of antiquities was located (inside the so-called Casino Capponi).

At the end of the 1620s Pietro da Cortona designed the scenic Villa del Pigneto (destroyed) for the Sacchetti family. This villa was the first truly baroque version of the type, and as such was a sort of template for the new stylistic guidelines. Its multitiered layout included terraced gardens and curving flights of steps, structures mixed with fountains and natural rock formations, a court opening onto a garden arranged along a series of staggered levels with a central recess, and statues and bas-reliefs in constant dialogue with plants and niches.

In 1630, the Pamphili family acquired a villa just outside the San Pancrazio Gate, and in 1644 it was adorned by the magnificent Casino del Belrespiro, designed by Alessandro Algardi and built by Giovanni Francesco Grimaldi. Lavishly decorated with ancient sculptures, it is built on a podium that elevates it over a geometric garden filled with ancient statues and sarcophagi. Reminiscent of both the Casino of Villa Borghese and the Villa del Pigneto, this mid-century villa represents a version of classicism as expressed within a baroque language.

By that time Rome was surrounded by a halo of villas of various sizes and levels of grandeur, most of them standing in areas that had not yet been completely built up. The period's best and most versatile artists and artisans were at work within these buildings. They eventually established a genre of architecture dedicated to the search for aesthetic pleasure that became an enduring model: casinos bursting with works of art, gardens in which views of illusionistic perspective alternated with scenes of uncultivated fields, panoramic views of the city that introduced the soul of the viewer to that particular taste for the picturesque that was to be developed more fully in the following century.

The Eighteenth-Century Palace: Between Grace and Nobility

In the eighteenth century, Rome rediscovered its creative vitality, which had waned during the last decades of the preceding century. Supported by a host of master masons, stone- and

native reworking of Borromini, he created a modern and picturesque style full of grace and nobility. Valvassori manipulated the traditional rules of composition and freely united the highly elaborate and original window decorations, taking a firm position against the classical side in the debate that was just getting under way in Rome and that would lead to neoclassicism.

In the same period Ferdinando Fuga (1699–1782) designed a series of magnificent palaces: the Consulta (1732–34), the Corsini (1736), and the Cenci-Bolognetti in Piazza del Gesù. In the Consulta he presented a model of elegant monumentality in which the orders on the palace are broken up by elegant sculptural groups, a form of virtuoso synthesis that nonetheless expressed the aspirations of the royal courts of Europe; the stairway is a reworking of the spectacular stairways of Naples. In Palazzo Corsini he created majestic, illusionistic spaces that became examples, together with those by Juvarra, for the works of Luigi Vanvitelli, who exercised his classicism in Rome by amplifying the facade (together with Nicola Salvi) of Bernini's Palazzo Chigi-Odescalchi.

Between the more fantastic expressions of the rococo and the advent of the neoclassical movement, important contributions to the evolution of style were made by minor architects, such as Niccolò Michetti (c. 1672–1759), who gave Palazzo Colonna near SS Apostoli its current appearance, directing workshops of imaginative and highly skilled stuccoworkers. Such workers also expressed themselves anonymously in complexes of typically rococo fascination like the Palazzo Grillo, with its Rainaldi-style nymphaeum and ceiling stuccoes of extraordinary richness (which have been attributed to an artist named Giuseppe Sardi), or the eighteenth-century apartments of Palazzo Barberini, or Palazzo Rondinini, restructured by Alessandro Dori at the middle of the century. Parting with the prevailing style of the preceding century, they went back to creating elaborate wall decorations, giving interiors a refined and welcoming elegance.

The last great Roman palace of the eighteenth century was built for Luigi and Romualdo Braschi, nephews of Pope Pius I. In 1790, they commissioned Cosimo Morelli (1732–1812) to build their palace, choosing his design over that of Luigi Valadier. The model chosen turned out to be based on the palaces of Sangallo, barely enlivened by a long horizontal balcony and a large cornice. Ignoring the neoclassical debate, Morelli made a building

stuccoworkers, artists of the highest quality, the architects of the eighteenth century adapted the language of the masters to new creations, devising a decorative sensibility that suited the new mood of Europe perfectly and came, once again, to influence it directly.

In this sense, the Roman training of Filippo Juvarra (1678–1736) during the first decade of the century was of great importance to his development. His principal employment in Rome was as a designer of stage sets, but architectural work includes completion of the loggia with niches of the Palazzetto Zuccari. The capricious style of the work, blended with tinges of classicism (he was a student of Carlo Fontana), was amplified in Juvarra's palaces in Turin, which became models for European palaces.

As a leading builder of civic architecture, Alessandro Specchi (1668–1729) created the Porto di Ripetta (destroyed), a docking area on the left bank of the Tiber in the center of Rome. In Palazzo Pichini (1710) in Piazza Farnese he designed a dramatic open stairway based on Neapolitan examples that is typically rococo, but in other palaces (such as Palazzo de Carolis on the Via del Corso, 1714–24, or Palazzo del Drago-Albani on the Via Quattro Fontane) he used a noble, classical language, a translation of the literary language of the Arcadian Academy.

From 1731 to 1733, Gabriele Valvassori (1683–1761) directed restoration work on Palazzo Doria Pamphili on the Via del Corso, creating one of the most beautiful facades in Rome. In an imagi-

whose style has been greatly undervalued by critics, who consider it the work of a conformist and thus an anachronistic structure. And yet it was precisely this building that became the model for the palaces built in Rome following Italy's unification (1870), for it can be seen as the prelude to the later revival of sixteenth-century style in the eclectic period of the nineteenth.

The age of the great noble palaces was already fast approaching its end during the first years of the eighteenth century, a time when financial resources were being focused on the construction of "residence homes," or apartment buildings, whose design is related to the evolution of middle-class society. Important early examples include the group of houses made by Filippo Raguzzini (c. 1680–1771) on Piazza di S. Ignazio (1727–35), a scenic expression of the light style of Borromini of the so-called Roman rococo (*barocchetto*) and a masterpiece of urban planning.

The Eighteenth-Century Villa

The economic conditions in Rome during the eighteenth century made the creation of suburban villas a truly unusual undertaking. Almost all the Roman villas of the eighteenth century were built immediately outside the Aurelian walls; the urban area within the walls had been taken over by the expansion of the city during the two preceding centuries. With rare exceptions, there were no monumental undertakings during the eighteenth century; in-

stead, existing gardens and villas were embellished. The few new structures that were built had a fancifully elegant character, but none of the opulence of the past. Several villas built during the late seventeenth century had hinted at this new situation. There was, for example, the Corsini Villa ai Quattro Venti (attributed to Simone Salvi, built around 1690, and today gone), which was no more than a simple pavilion completely enclosed in a vertical facade with a bizarre crown, open dramatically at the bottom with an arch, but almost paradoxically static. There was also the Villa d'Alibert; this, too, was very small and completely enclosed in its loggia facade, more stage set than building.

In 1715 Cardinal Giovanni Battista began work on Villa Patrizi (demolished in the last century), which adopted a grandiose scheme, in this case inspired by the fanciful Villa Benedetti, or "del Vascello" (meaning "the vessel," because its front resembled the prow of a ship). This bizarre creation mixing naturalistic and illusionistic elements was built in 1663 by the architect-painter Basilio Bricci (1621–1692) with the assistance of his sister Plautilla Bricci (1616–after 1690). Recent scholarship suggests that Plautilla, the first female architect whose reputation has survived to today, may have been the true designer, but her contribution (like the date of her death) has been forgotten. The architect of the Villa Patrizi, Sebastiano Cipriani, had been one of the leading interpreters of rococo architecture in Rome, and together with Alessandro Specchi he had broken free of the academic restraints

of the late seventeenth century to create fantastic works within Borromini's style of frameworks and capricious outlines.

Another monumental creation, and the last great villa in eighteenth-century Rome, was Villa Albani, built at the middle of the century for Cardinal Alessandro Albani, nephew of Pope Clement XI, a great collector of antiquities, and patron of Johann Winckelmann. It was designed by Carlo Marchionnni to display the collection of marbles and follows a horizontal scheme that emphasizes a new relationship (almost one of submission) with nature. In that sense it is in keeping with the nascent poetics reflecting the picturesque and sublime aspects of nature. With its academic rhythm, it represents a moment in the history of architecture between a still "Arcadian" classicism (showing the influence of Fuga) and the movement that, driven on by the new ideas of Wincklemann and Piranesi, moved toward the neoclassical.

Other eighteenth-century buildings seem far more modest in terms of size. Bosco Parrasio on the Janiculum, where the literary Arcadian Academy met, is really no more than a picturesque series of staircases and terraces with a small amphitheater. It was designed in 1725 by Antonio Canevari (1681–1764), who drew inspiration from Rome's Spanish Steps (1723–26), a contemporary work by Francesco de' Sanctis (fl. 1717–26). Also worthy of mention is the Coffee House of the Quirinal gardens,

designed by Fuga in 1741–43 as the completion of the sixteenth- and seventeenth-century garden. It is a masterpiece of eighteenth-century grace, an expression of the "international" style of the late baroque.

On a more moderate, less classical scale, there is the Villa Gentili (now Dominici) by Filippo Raguzzini, master of the Roman *barocchetto*, which is a structural reworking of ideas from Borromini. There is then the Villa Chigi (1763), which from the outside looks like a simple, slightly modernized farmhouse, while on the inside it is an absolute jewel of decoration in stucco and frescoes, art that balances between the rococo and a new picturesque "English" style. This is most visible in the Tebaide rooms, painted by Francesco Nubale with illusionistic scenes of wild rocky landscapes peopled by hermits.

The centuries-long history of the study and construction of villas in Rome concludes in 1764 with the only architectural complex made by Giovanni Battista Piranesi (1720–1778). This is the villa of the Knights of Malta on the Aventine Hill. The spectacular encircling wall, crowned by obelisks, vases, inscriptions, and trophies, takes and refashions Fuga's noble *barocchismo* so as to project it into a visionary, almost dreamy realm populated by ancient citations reworked with an almost Borrominian flair, opening the way not just to the imminent neoclassical style but, even more, to the psychological pathos of European Romanticism.

Palaces of the Renaissance

Francesco Salviati, detail showing
the frescoes from the chapel of
Palazzo della Cancelleria.

Palazzo della Cancelleria

To the side of the great theater of Pompey, just to the north of the barracks for one of the squadrons (the Greens) of charioteers that served the circus games, a primitive center of religious worship known as the *titlus* arose early in the Christian era. In the fourth century, Pope Damasus I (364–84) enlarged this structure with the addition of a church in memory of the martyrdom of San Lorenzo. A building was constructed to the side of this to house the Sacred Books of the Roman church. A millennium later, toward the end of the fifteenth century, this palace came to occupy a central place in the large-scale plans for renewing the city of Rome devised by Pope Sixtus IV, who hoped to restore Rome to its former glory. The humanistic ideals of the Renaissance reached their fullest expression in Rome under Sixtus IV, and this palace, which belonged to the pope's nephew Raffaele Riario, came to represent the current of humanist thought that had evolved in Urbino. The Campus Martius, praised by the Greek author Strabo for combining natural beauty with manmade splendor,

After the reconstruction of the palace, the central doorway was redesigned in 1589 by Domenico Fontana for the Cardinal of Montaldo.

OPPOSITE: The coat of arms of the Della Rovere family was placed by Giulio Della Rovere on a corner of the palace.

had declined such that it was little more than a formless maze of meandering alleys; the "redeeming labors" of Sixtus sought to transform this area of the city. The stately shape of the palace fit with the ambitious plans of reconstruction. As indicated by recent archaeological excavations in the courtyard, the palace covered only partially the site of the ancient temple, which faced a different direction and was a different size, but had been incorporated in the palace by Riario, making the palace the largest, most impressive, and most highly refined in fifteenth-century Rome. Although not a priest, Raffaele Riario was made cardinal of San Giorgio at Velabro in 1477, a nomination that earned him the name Cardinal San Giorgio. In 1483, his authority was extended to include the area of San Lorenzo in Damaso, and he received the use, for all his natural life, of the contiguous palace, which he immediately set about modernizing. The destruction of the older building and the church itself began in 1484, year of the death of Sixtus IV, and according to an inscription on the facade the work was completed in 1495. The final decorations were completed after Raffaele Riario's nomination to bishop of Ostia in 1511. Only seventeen years old when made cardinal, Raffaele Riario experienced a lifetime of success, although he did find himself facing great peril

twice in his life. On both occasions, he was imprisoned for conspiracy: the first during the Pazzi conspiracy of 1478 and then, forty years later, during the Petrucci conspiracy under Leo X. At that time the palace was taken away from the Riario family and made into the

offices of the papal chancery (*cancelleria*). Riario's portrait appears in a fresco by Melozzo da Forlì that is now in the Vatican's picture gallery and also in Raphael's fresco *The Mass of Bolsena* in the Stanze della Segnatura. He was an ambitious Renaissance man. He rebuilt the palace of

building. Pietro Aretino, in a letter of November 22, 1537, to the "Magnifico Messer Giovanni Bolani" confirms this, writing, "I've spent entire days hearing how San Giorgio won 70,000 ducts from Franceschetto and how, with those winnings, he built the palace in Campo di Fiori."

Various themes, such as the *Beheading of Battista* and the *Forge of the Vulcan,* were narrated in a cycle treated with uniform style and embellished by rich decorative elements in the frames around the scenes.

San Damaso, had the church incorporated into the building itself, following the precedent of the Palazzo Venezia, as though it were a Palatine chapel. An anecdote narrated in the *Diario* of Stefano Infessura recounts how the cardinal won the sum of 14,000 ducats from Franceschetto Cybo playing dice and how, when the pope instructed him to give the money back to the loser, he explained that he could not, since he had already spent it all on wood, bricks, and stone for the construction of the

So rapidly did the work proceed that by 1492 the ground-floor shops on Via del Pellegrino had been rented. (The Cancelleria was the first Renaissance palace to revive the ancient Roman custom of having shops on the ground floor of city homes.) The facade, entirely covered in travertine with its floors marked off by rows of classical pilasters, was completed three years later. The main portal was radically changed in 1589, being flanked by two granite columns according to plans by

Domenico Fontana on commission of the illustrious great grandson of Sixtus V, Alessandro Peretti, then vice chancellor. Given the lack of direct references in surviving documents, the architect responsible for this work cannot be properly identified, although he was certainly of the first rank. Vasari gives credit to the theory that Bramante was entrusted with the technical supervision of the work, acting in the role of advisor: "His reputation increasing, he was one of the eminent artists consulted about the palace of San Giorgio . . . which, though improved afterward, was and still is considered a comfortable and magnificent abode for its size." The theory that Bramante was in some way involved is made impossible by the dates involved: he was in Lombardy until 1496. The long, travertine facade and rhythmic spacing of the paired pilasters testify instead to the mathematical search for harmony based on the golden section that was typical of the leading Roman architect of the fifteenth century, Baccio Pontelli (1450–ca. 1494), to whom art historian C. L. Frommel makes a convincing attribution. The solidly monumental courtyard extends the entire width of the building with a double order of arches topped by an attic in brick and with pilasters and windows in an orderly arrangement based on the ducal palace of Urbino. Michelangelo

was familiar with Cardinal San Giorgio's home and admired its sense of harmony; as Vasari reports, he sold the cardinal a sculpture of a sleeping cupid. The motif of the wild rose, emblem of the Riario family, appears in several places on the facade. The rooms had wooden coffered

ceilings, carved in a design inspired by those of ancient Roman vaults, and painted friezes with the cardinal's coat of arms. The work of decorating the palace was

The elongated figures in the coffers of the vault reflect the diffusion of mannerist elements, of which Salviati was one of the most skilled interpreters.

PAGES 40-41: The decoration of the Salone dei Cento Giorni, allegedly finished in one hundred days, was begun in the summer of 1546 by Giorgio Vasari.

taken up again around the middle of the century. Francesco Salviati painted a *Beheading of St. John the Baptist* and *Martyrdom of St. Lawrence* in the Pallio Chapel. Perino del Vaga worked in the Sala della Torre, which gave onto the garden. The Sala dei Cento Giorni was made by Vasari and a large team of assistants; it was finished in the summer of 1546, supposedly in 100 days. In this work the famous compiler of the *Lives* created a large manneristic complex based on an erudite and cultured iconographic repertory conceived by Paolo Giovio, who chose as the theme the glorification of the deeds of Pope Paul III. The allegorical figures were skillfully arranged along a stairway using false perspective. The palace experienced a new period of glory during the early years of the eighteenth century thanks to the theater (no longer in existence) that Filippo Juvarra (1678–1736) designed for Cardinal Pietro Ottoboni, a lover of theater and a patron of the arts, creating a special place for musical performances. In his Italian memoirs, the French magistrate and writer Charles de Brosses (1709–1777) tells of a performance of the *Armide* by Lully, in 1739, given before an audience of prelates and crowned heads, ambassadors and grand dames. On February 9, 1849, the Roman republic was proclaimed from the palace. In accordance with the Lateran Treaty, the Cancelleria enjoys extraterritorial status.

Palazzo Massimo alle Colonne

The Massimo family traces its lineage farther back through the centuries than any other Roman family, claiming an uninterrupted line that begins with the origin of the city itself. The family's fortified home, thrown together with medieval disorder and built upon later, was destroyed in 1527 during the terrible sack of Rome that threw its dark shadow over the towering ideals of humanism.

A few years later, the Sienese architect Baldassare Peruzzi was commissioned to reconstruct the central palace, and his work on this building came to represent the greatest expression of his architectural skills. Peruzzi himself had suffered a great deal during the sack of Rome, for, as Vasari relates, he was taken prisoner by the Spanish; "he lost not only everything he had but was in addition abused, for, since he had an imposing, noble, and elegant manner, they took him for some prelate in disguise or someone capable of paying a heavy fine. . . . once free [he] set out for Porto Ercole and Siena, but on the way he was robbed and stripped of everything; he arrived in Siena in a shirt." Peruzzi's client for this

A bronze model of the palace showing the facade made by Baldassare Peruzzi between 1532 and 1536. The design employs elements based on ancient buildings, which the architect had avidly studied, assembling a repertory of citations gathered from the remains of imperial Rome. The smooth rustication of the facade includes a Doric portico on the ground floor with elegant plaster decoration. By making the facade curve slightly, the architect was able to respect the law according to which Via Papalis could not be more than five yards wide at its widest point.

work was Pietro Massimo, eldest son of the rich merchant Domenico, killed in the sack, who had in his will left his three sons three adjoining buildings.

The building stands on the site of the ancient odeon, a theater for musical contests, of the emperor Domitian, and its facade follows the semicircular curve of the ancient building's *cavea*, which, according to the *Regionaries*, ancient descriptions of the city, had seats for ten thousand people. As in a symphony of his own, Peruzzi orchestrated the ornamental elements, which are skillfully applied to a structure with the clean lines recommended by Donato Bramante. Highly original in his methods, Peruzzi was, in a sense, a perfect incarnation of the figure of the humanist architect who studies relics from the ancient world with tireless curiosity, seeking to understand their innermost harmonies. Thanks to the efforts of his powerful protector Agostino Chigi, he had entered Bramante's workshop as a young man, and there he had drawn "marvelous fruit," as Vasari reports. For the Massimo palace he drew on his entire repertory of ideas gleaned from ancient ruins, including those he had studied firsthand. The home of the Massimo family stands out from the grandiose palaces that were being built throughout Rome in those same years, for it clearly conveys a sense of human dimensions and human scale

as its basic measure in the proportions of the spaces and the pilasters.

The wonderful portico, decorated with elegant stuccowork and supported by the six Doric columns that give the palace its name (*alle Colonne*), leads to the first courtyard, which re-creates

the Vitruvian model of the *vestibulum*. Peruzzi was forced to resort to some odd expedients in his efforts to preserve as much as possible of the damaged original building. He maintained existing walls in an attempt to hold down costs. The dark vestibule, covered by a barrel vault decorated with stuccoes and bas-reliefs, was probably made after Peruzzi's death in 1536 by the members of his workshop. Inexpensive materials were used with exquisite dexterity, with the central scene of shields, helmets, and breastplates pulled by an ele-

phant and flanked by the good-luck Fortune on one side and adverse Fate on the other. In an obsessive effort to reconstruct the ancient past, Peruzzi planned a dining room for the ground floor and indicated it on his designs as a *triclinium*. Dating to the same period is the scene of Venus surrounded by grotesques. Like a true ancient Greek peristyle, the first courtyard was decorated with reliefs and statues. A century later, Carlo Camillo Massimo installed a small nymphaeum built to replace the original ancient fountain.

The historical palace was built by Pietro Massimo, father of Domenico, and decorated in chiaroscuro and carved on the facade. This fifteenth-century building survived the destruction of the sack of Rome and was celebrated for having been the seat of the oldest Roman press, founded in 1467 by the Germans Pannartz and Sweynhaim. The frescoes, today in poor condition, were created by Polidoro da Caravaggio and Maturino of Florence.

The Massimo family had assembled a large collection of stone inscriptions, ancient "curiosities," statues, funeral pillars, and bas-reliefs, and many of these are today displayed among the stucco decorations by Peruzzi in the palace's two courtyards and in the vault of the entrance hall.

The second courtyard, most of which dates to the seventeenth century, preserves the sole surviving element of the ancient odeon, mixed in among the collection of various other "curiosities" that the Massimos, like most Renaissance families, collected. A stairway adorned by marble relics led up to the frescoed loggia of the first floor, right up to the threshold of a door crowned by the coat of arms of the Massimo family. The Palazzo di Pirro, built for Pietro's brother Angelo, was connected to the rebuilt Palazzo del Portico, making it possible to move from the rooms of one palace to those of the other without interruption.

In the great hall Daniele da Volterra made frieze decorations of the life of the legendary Fabius Maximus, and Perino del Vaga covered the walls of the side rooms with grotesques and scenes taken from the *Aeneid*. These filled the space with a combination of pagan hedonism and refined elegance, the ideal setting, a century later, for the learned conversations conducted by Carlo Camillo Masssimo, who met here with his friend Nicolas Poussin, giving the learned painter new inspirations for the highly intellectual themes of his works, at least according to the biographer and art critic Giovanni Pietro Bellori. The prince was a friend of Velázquez, and his fascinating library became a center for meetings of the most celebrated scholars of his time.

An elegant staircase leads to the *piano nobile* and the great hall with its coffered ceiling and frieze decorations by Daniele da Volterra. These decorations narrate the life of Fabius Maximus, the legendary founder of the Roman family which is said to date back to the very birth of the *Urbs*. Four Roman statues are arranged along the long walls.

These rooms were not only the site of conversations, but also of miracles, as recalled by the votive chapel of St. Philip Neri, dedicated to that saint who, in 1583, succeeded in resuscitating for several hours a young member of the family who had been given up for dead. The anniversary of this miracle is celebrated in the palace every March 16.

A famous collection of paintings was kept in the palace during the seventeenth century, but was almost immediately dispersed, and the palace's primary importance has long remained its emblematic standing within the works of Baldassare Peruzzi, being, in effect, his last testament.

The palace was well known to Rome's citizens. Before the opening in 1880 of Corso Vittorio Emanuel, which caused the tearing apart of this Renaissance quarter and its principal artery (the so-called Via Papalis), the stretch that joined the Chiesa Nuovo to Sant'Andrea della Valle was occupied by smaller buildings, broken up by narrow streets that led the pedestrian toward the natural curve of the palace.

The urban fabric of the little piazza behind the palace is still intact, as is the Massimo family's Palazzetto Istoriato, with its facade decorated with monochrome frescoes by Polidoro da Caravaggio; it, too, is connected to the two palaces that the brothers Piero and Angelo built. The exterior decoration, made in honor of the marriage of Angelo Massimo to Antonietta Planca Incoronati, presents scenes of the marriage of the Virgin, the life of Esther, and the murder of Holofernes. Nearby, from 1467 until it was destroyed in 1527, was the site of the Roman printing firm of Arnold Pannartz and Konrad Sweynheim, who published works by Cicero and St. Augustine. Mail coaches and couriers once set off from this piazza on routes leading even to foreign countries, part of a service directly related to the Massimo family, since a Massimo was postmaster general of the pontifical post in the eighteenth century.

PAGES 48–49: The Stanza Egizia was made in the *retour d'Egypte* style, which came into vogue across Europe following Napoleon's Egyptian campaign, and presents views of the Nile and the pyramids flanked by sphinxes and pharaohs.

RIGHT: The palace's votive chapel, open to the public every year on March 16, recalls the miracle performed by St. Philip Neri when he resuscitated a young member of the Massimo family after several hours. In the chapel are a panel by Nicola di Antonio d'Ancona, including a *Virgin with Four Saints*, a painting by Niccolò Pomarancio depicting the miracle, and cult objects.

Palazzo Farnese

The supreme elegance of this stately palace is the result of contributions from the most celebrated architects of its day. In working on this palace, those great artists provided the Farnese family with a residence truly worthy of its rank.

The Farnese family had come by that rank, and its power, quite rapidly, far faster, in fact, than any other family. During the sixteenth century, the family amassed a colossal fortune, along with incomparable fame. Most of this came to them by way of the sword, but there were also the contributions of a woman, Giulia, sister of Alessandro Farnese and one of Pope Alexander VI's favorite mistresses. It was Alessandro, first as a fearsome cardinal and then as Pope Paul III (1534–49), who built this palace, its magnificence designed as an unmistakable expression of the dominant role he intended his papacy to play within Roman aristocracy, based on a centralized court capable of imposing its will in both politics and in art.

Cardinal Alessandro turned to Antonio da Sangallo the Younger, whose interests centered precisely on the

The Farnese Palace was built by Cardinal Alessandro Farnese, future Pope Paul III, who began work on it before his nomination to the pontificate. The original project was entrusted to Antonio da Sangallo the Younger, but it later came to involve the leading architects of the period. The windows on the first floor of the majestic facade are topped by alternating arched and triangular pediments; those on the third floor have triangular pediments only.

central theme of the palace. From 1514 until his death in 1546, he held the monopoly on all Roman work at a certain level, having assembled an efficient workshop that he directed personally. Crystal clear in its structure and truly imposing, the palace for the Farnese family perfectly expressed Alessandro's solid nobility as a passionate humanist and collector of medallions and marbles, gemstones and coins.

The palace that Sangallo designed for the cardinal was enlarged and embellished after Alessandro was elected pope as Paul III, in 1534, since he himself, Vasari says, demanded "a palace fit not for a cardinal, but for a pope." Following Sangallo's death in 1546 many artists contributed to this transformation, from Vasari to Perino del Vaga and Sebastiano del Piombo. By a twist of fate, in 1547 the pope entrusted the work to Michelangelo, who was a dedicated foe of what he himself derided as the "Sangallo gang." Michelangelo harbored much resentment of Sangallo, not just for having monopolized the most important commissions but also because he was convinced that Sangallo had hatched endless intrigues to keep him out of the city and thus prevent him from working there.

In the Farnese, Michelangelo contributed to the completion of the top floor, making it taller and topping it with a powerful cornice. He designed the arcaded window beside the main entrance and the third order, more capricious, along the courtyard, for which Sangallo had drawn his inspiration from the decorative system of the Colosseum. The columned atrium designed by Sangallo, as well as the first two orders of the courtyard, reflected Alessandro's classical taste. In fact, during those same years the cardinal had promoted excavations on the Palatine and in the Roman Forum. The beautiful loggia looking out over the Tiber, on the back of the palace, was designed by Giacomo della Porta.

Francesco Salviati (1510–63) probably began the decoration of the Salotto Dipinto in 1554. The artist's stay in France from 1555 to 1557 interrupted the work, but he went back to it on his return to Rome. The theme of the cycle of decorations is the glorification of the Farnese family, particularly the role of peacemaker carried out by Paul III, a great statesman in the service of the church. The pope's deeds, as well as those of Ranuccio Farnese, general of the papal forces under Pope Eugenius IV, are narrated in the foreground along the walls of the hall, the scenes alternating with allegorical references to ancient or mythological tales or personages enclosed within faux draperies. The complex spatial organization creates a kind of dialogue among the various scenes, which thus are compared and blended, giving rise to unexpected revelations and intriguing cross-references. The lively fantasy, subtle reasoning, and skillful decorations of the lateral motifs display Salviati's extraordinary inventive talents. After his death, in 1563, his work was completed by Taddeo Zuccaro.

The great military commander Alessandro Farnese, who had spent his life serving Philip II of Spain and who was compared by his contemporaries to Alexander the Great, died in 1592, leaving the ducal titles to Parma and Piacenca to his first-born son, another Ranuccio. His second-born son, Odoardo,

The atrium of the palace, by Antonio da Sangallo the Younger, is divided by red granite columns into three naves, reflecting the archaeological interests of Alessandro Farnese, who, during those same years, sponsored archaeological excavations on the Palatine Hill and in the Roman Forum. Roman busts in the niches mark off the space, which leads to the porticoed courtyard.

became cardinal at seventeen and set about completing the decoration of the Roman palace. The double-story Sala Grande, yet to be decorated, gave the young heir the opportunity to continue the glorification of his father begun by Salviati. By then, in the years around the end of the century, the custom of narrating a family's exploits had become widespread among the noble families of Europe. On July 17, 1593, Odoardo wrote to his brother the Duke Ranuccio in Parma, asking him to send him copies of the eight Flemish paintings presenting the great deeds of Alessandro, since they could be used as models (they never arrived). The artistic panorama of Rome was enriched by the new and decisive presence of Annibale Carracci, who on the invitation of Odoardo moved from Bologna to take part in the decorations. He began with the cardinal's private studiolo in 1595, setting aside the Sala Grande. Annibale had brought a highly skilled workshop with him to Rome, and his arrival injected a swirl of new ideas into the capital, by then growing weary of the tired state of mannerism. A considerable number of Emilian artists followed him in the next few years, eventually forming the nucleus of artists who later gave life to the baroque revolution. The decorative program of the studiolo, known as the Camerino, was worked out by the prince's librarian, Fulvio Orsini, following a

theme that set the Muses against famous warriors. The stories of Hercules and Ulysses were meant as allegorical allusions to the victory of virtue over temptation.

Pleased with the work, and also well aware that the palace inaugurated an important turn toward the classical,

The frescoes in the gallery by the brothers Annibale and Agostino Carracci present the loves of the gods and end, at the center, with the episode of the *Triumph of Bacchus and Ariadne*, an exaltation of profane love presented with a

naturalism that is a prelude to the baroque. The palace's ceiling marked the waning of the complex allegories of mannerism, and the birth of a new pictorial language, classical and in tune with the hedonism of the chosen themes.

the cardinal immediately entrusted Annibale Carracci with the decoration of the ceiling of the gallery, which he worked on with the assistance of his brother Agostino and a large team of assistants, including Domenichino (Domenico Zampieri) and Giovanni Lanfranco. Large paintings in faux frames narrated the loves of the gods, the dominant theme, in keeping with Virgil's maxim *"Omnia vincit amor et nos cedemus amori"* ("Love conquers all; let us yield to its power"). The actual author of the plan is not known with any certainty, but it seems likely that the cardinal himself and Fulvio Orsini worked it out together as the frescoes were worked on, being finally completed in 1597. Herms and atlantes in grisaille work frame the spirited paintings, which are enlivened by the pink tones of the putti and encircled by tondos with faux bronze reliefs with green patinas. The centerpiece in the middle of the vault is the *Triumph of Bacchus and Ariadne*, a triumph of profane and sensual love, illustrating the mythical story with the greatest realism. In a thorough and decisive way, Annibale surpassed the late-mannerist fondness for complex allegories, captious reasoning, and moralizing references to present a spontaneous narration of classical fables. From the day it was first uncovered before the enchanted eyes of Pope Clement VIII and his nephew Cardinal Pietro Aldobrandini until the end of the eigh-

The Sala Grande, which is two stories high, has no painted decoration. At its center is a monumental fireplace by Guglielmo della Porta, dated 1554, which is flanked by statues of *Abundance* and *Peace*, originally made by Della Porta as decorations for Paul III's tomb in St. Peter's basilica. The wall niches hold Roman busts, and the room has an extraordinary coffered ceiling.

teenth century, Carracci's decoration in the gallery was ranked among the greatest pictorial displays, equaled only by the Vatican Stanze and the Sistine Chapel. It was painting suitable to satisfy the refined taste of its noble client and to express the emerging hedonism that was bringing an end to the Tridentine reforms (promulgated during the Council of Trent), which had suffocated the city and restricted the imaginations of its artists. Packed by Odoardo with antique sculptures from the famous Farnese collection, the gallery brought to shining life a new language, happy and carefree, perfectly in keeping with the secular

A splendid eighteenth-century tapestry hangs in the corridor.

OPPOSITE: One of the famous baroque coffered ceilings of the Farnese palace.

subjects of the chosen theme. Once again the palace was in the vanguard of inventiveness, offering the world a view of the still-nascent baroque style. •

After the death, in 1731, of the last Farnese of the Neapolitan line of the Bourbons, the library and archaeological collection were taken to Naples, and the palace began a slow decline from which it was rescued only in 1874, when it was rented to the ambassador of France.

The Salone dei Fasti, decorated with frescoes by Francesco Salviati and Taddeo Zuccaro between 1549 and 1556, exalts the glory of the Farnese family and the political deeds of Paul III. The deeds of the pope and those of Ranuccio Farnese alternate with mythological scenes and scenes based on ancient history.

Palazzo Orsini Savelli

The theater of Marcellus stood at the heart of the ancient city, in the monumental zone where enormous buildings crowded side by side along the city blocks, forming a towering spectacle that must have astonished and stupefied the foreigners who made their way into the great *Urbs* by one of its sixteen gates. The impressive theater, begun by Caesar and finished by Augustus between 13 and 11 B.C., was named for Augustus's beloved nephew Marcus Claudius Marcellus, whom Augustus had adopted as his son. He was considered to be Augustus's intended heir, but he died prematurely at twenty-one years of age (and was recalled by Virgil in several famous verses of the *Aeneid*). The auditorium of the theater had room for fifteen thousand spectators. The exterior was covered with travertine marble and had forty-one arcades; over the keystone of each arch was a large theatrical mask of carved marble. Today the theater is without its stage, but the lower part of the ancient building is still well preserved. During the Middle Ages the area around the theater was the most densely populated of the city.

According to Suetonius, Julius Caesar began work on a theater in an effort to eclipse the theater of Pompey, which was then enjoying much fame. Caesar's theater, which stood near the Flaminian Circus, was designed for fifteen thousand spectators and was second in size only to the Colosseum. Interrupted by Caesar's death, work on the theater was completed by Augustus, who dedicated it in 13 B.C. to his nephew Marcus Claudius Marcellus. Because of its strategic location, the monument was fortified during the Middle Ages and became the residence for various powerful Roman families, including the Pierleoni and then the Savelli, who gave their name to the palace built on the site in the early sixteenth century.

PAGES 68–69: The house that Baldassare Peruzzi built for Cardinal Savelli in the first half of the sixteenth century was designed to give that prelate the rare opportunity of competing with a classical monument. Greatly reworked during the nineteenth century, little remains of Peruzzi's creation except the height of the stories. The staircase leading to the apartment on the top floor was restored by Tommaso Buzzi using a profusion of polychrome marbles.

Since it dominated the three bridges that joined the city to the Tiber Island and thus to Trastevere it was of strategic importance. During the thirteenth century the building was included in the property of the aristocratic Fabii family, as indicated by the ancient name Monte Fabiorum, although the Pierleoni are later cited as the principal owners. A century later, in 1361, the theater is listed among the properties of the Savelli family, who early on built a fortified palace on that spot from which to dominate their holdings. These extended to the Aventine, where they had a new residence built, a building that can probably be identified with the old imperial palace of Otto III. Two future popes were born and lived inside those fortified walls: Cencio Savelli, future Pope Honorius III, and Giacomo Savelli, elected pope as Honorius IV. An interesting document dated February 24, 1279, includes the will of Cardinal Giacomo Savelli, who names as his heirs Leone and Giovanni, confirming that the building belonged to the Savelli family on that date. As Pope Honorius IV (1285–87) he brought great prestige to the family, particularly as a result of the important role he played in beautifying the city, bringing back a sense of splendor and opulence to the court that helped raise Rome to new glories. Leone and Giovanni were granted titles as marshals of the Holy Roman Church and guardians of the conclave. The power of the medieval noble houses began to wane, but the Savelli house maintained much of its power and glory until the sixteenth century. In 1535 they had a new palace built atop the ancient fortifications, and as architect they chose Baldassare Peruzzi

Thanks to the careful restoration work performed by the architect Tommaso Buzzi, the rooms again have much of their original baroque splendor. In the foreground is the fascinating bronze and Oriental jasper table that Alessandro Algari made for Scipione Borghese in the seventeenth century; on the rear wall is a polyptych by Matteo di Pacino including a Coronation of the Virgin, dated 1370. The giltwood chairs were originally made in the eighteenth century for the Chigi Palace; the coffered ceiling dates to the seventeenth century.

(1481–1536), who was in Rome that year for the last time in his life. Peruzzi had dedicated much time to the close study of ancient ruins, seeking to understand the secrets of their harmonies. Above the ancient theater he built a two-story structure composed of three rectangular wings facing a central courtyard, an arrangement that is no longer visible because it was thoroughly altered by nineteenth-century renovations. The size of both floors probably dates to the Peruzzi design, however. The main entrance opened in a high wall with battlements that served to protect the building from flooding of the Tiber. Cardinal Giulio Savelli assembled a famous collection of ancient sculpture in the halls of the palace, which served as the setting for meetings of a circle of artists and scholars led by the humanist Onofrio Panvinio (1530–1568).

When the last heir of the ancient Savelli family died in 1712, the palace came into the possession of the Sforza Cesarini. It then became the property of Domenico Orsini, prince of Gravina. During the eighteenth century minor artists decorated the *piano nobile* and nineteenth-century architects thoroughly erased what remained of the architectural elements designed by Peruzzi, reworking the areas created by that great Sienese artist.

From earliest times until the first years of this century, a cattle market was held near the theater. Ancient records indicate that the Savelli family itself rented out the ground floor to butchers and artisans from the thirteenth century onward, and chronicles from 1920 speak of little shops doing a lively business under the ancient arches.

The rooms of Palazzo Savelli are splendidly appointed with textiles and antiquities. The sixteenth- and seventeenth-century tapestries are noteworthy.

Castel Sant'Angelo

The emperor Hadrian (A.D. 76–138) was a man of great learning and foresight. Highly gifted, an accomplished poet and musician, he was interested in such diverse subjects as archaeology, philosophy, mathematics, and, in particular, architecture. A great builder, he adorned provincial cities with arches and directed the construction of defensive walls, notably across the narrow part of the island of Great Britain. He traveled widely, spending fully twelve years, more than half his reign, away from Rome. Troubled by illness during his last years, he dedicated himself to putting his affairs in order, along with those of the empire. This included the preparation of a suitable place for his burial. The mausoleum of Augustus had been opened to receive the ashes of the emperor Nerva, but was now full; the remains of Trajan, who had died without heirs, had been laid to rest in the base of the column erected in his honor. A new structure was needed, and the building that Hadrian had constructed became the mausoleum of the Antonine dynasty. For the site for his tomb, Hadrian

The emperor Hadrian made careful arrangements for his place of burial, and his tomb, used for the emperors of the Antonine line, was inaugurated in A.D. 139. Hadrian's tomb survives as part of the complex of Castel Sant'Angelo, the structure that is the result of the tomb's transformation into a medieval fortress.

OPPOSITE: Pope Gregory I dedicated the building to the warrior archangel Michael in 590 after having a vision of the archangel sheathing his sword over Hadrian's tomb during a procession to pray for the end of a plague. Raffaello da Montelupo made a stone angel that stood atop the building until 1753, when it was replaced by a bronze angel with outspread wings made by Pietro van Verschaffelt. Today, Raffaello's angel is in the Cortile dell'Angelo.

The loggia was made early in the sixteenth century, probably by Bramante, and was the first of a series of alterations made to the fortress for the purpose of making it suitable for papal apartments. Those apartments were then richly furnished and fitted out with the most "modern" conveniences.

chose an area on the right bank of the Tiber River, opposite the Campus Martius, the quiet area of the gardens of Domitia. The emperor Nero had embellished this area of imperial gardens with parks and fountains. Hadrian had the area connected to the Campus Martius by way of a new bridge, the Pons Aelius. This bridge was dedicated in A.D. 134.

Spared damage during the great upheavals that over the centuries afflicted the city of the Caesars, the monument, known as Hadrian's Mausoleum or Hadrian's Mole and today part of Castel Sant'Angelo, was inaugurated in 139, one year after the emperor's death at Baiae. It was built in accordance with the three-tier design of early Italian and Roman tradition, the same design that had been used earlier for the tomb of Augustus, and much of it was faced in white marble. Its

three tiers included a broad podiumlike base, atop which stood the main drum, the mausoleum proper, containing the funerary chamber itself, which in turn was topped by a smaller pedestal and drum. The main drum was decorated with pilasters and a frieze with bucrania and garlands, fragments of which are today preserved in the castle's museum. The sixth-century historian Procopius of Caesarea mentions marble equestrian statues placed on the four corners of the base, while gilt peacocks, today in the courtyard of the Pigna in the Vatican, stood inside the enclosure on pillars of peperino. A four-horse chariot guided by the emperor stood atop the final drum, and the main drum was covered with a mound of earth planted with a grove of cypresses and evergreen bushes in keeping with ancient Etruscan tradition. The vast funerary cham-

ber was located at the center of the main drum and was reached by way of a spiral ramp that was originally dressed with marble slabs and decorated with pilasters. The chamber itself contained the remains of Hadrian, his wife, Sabina, his adopted son, L. Aelius Caesar, and later emperors, the last of whom was Caracalla, killed in A.D. 217. In 271, facing the threat of barbarian invasions, the emperor Aurelian incorporated the monument as a bastion in the famous walls he had built around the city. By an irony of fate, with the passage of centuries, the tomb of a man who had been a peaceful and wise emperor became the setting for blood-baths and turbulent clashes of arms; it retained its basic elements but changed appearance, being gradually transformed into a fearsome castle protected by the warrior archangel Michael. The day

came when it truly lived up to its description as "the most forbidding and impregnable defense of the ancient world."

By the end of the fourth century, the tomb had become a bridgehead fortress. In 537, serving as a bulwark in the defenses against barbarians, it held out during the year-long siege by the Ostrogoth king Witiges. Procopius relates how during the long siege many of the statues atop the tomb were broken into pieces and hurled over the walls onto the heads of the enemy. In 590 Rome was struck by plague, and Pope Gregory I (590–604) led a penitential procession through the city to pray for its cessation; hundreds died along the route, but the pope saw a vision of the archangel Michael sheathing his sword in the air over Hadrian's tomb, which the pope took as a sign that their prayers had been answered. A chapel was built on the tomb, and its name eventually changed to Castel Sant'Angelo.

For more than a thousand years, the giant tomb of Hadrian served to protect the city. Strategically vital during the Middle Ages because of its proximity to the most sacred site of all Christendom, the tomb of St. Peter, the castle had enormous appeal to popes, who longed to possess it. When he arrived in Rome in 800, Charlemagne had defensive walls built joining the ancient tomb to the Lateran Palace, which was also near his palace. After Charlemagne's death and

that of Leo III, the pope who had supported and crowned him, the Romans rebelled, doing much damage to the dangerous citadel; it was later rebuilt by Pope Leo IV (847–55) to face the danger of Saracen attack.

During the closing centuries of the Middle Ages the

BELOW: The bees carved on this decorative ball are the heraldic symbol of the Barberini family, which provided Rome with cardinals and a pope (Urban VIII). The Barberini were known for their lavish patronage: no family's symbol appears more often in St. Peter's basilica than their bees. Here, the bees record one of the many restoration projects done to modernize the castle.

OPPOSITE: The Cortile dell'Angelo is named for the statue of the archangel made by Raffaello da Montelupo, which is displayed there. The courtyard gives access to the apartments of Clement VII, and is decorated with the coat of arms of Paul III.

castle passed into the hands of powerful noble families, becoming the scene of conspiracies and murderous feuds. In 928 Pope John X was suffocated in one of the castle's dungeons by order of the Italian noblewoman Marozia, daughter of the Roman consul Theophylact and his wife Theodora; in 932 Marozia married Ugo of Provence in the chapel dedicated to the archangel; in 974 Theodora's son had Pope Benedict VI killed, also by suffocation. The detailed account of the city left by a bishop of Lucca in 1090 relates that the building was then owned by the Crescenzi family. Pope Nicholas III (1277–80) undertook the first attempts to transfer the

papal see from the Lateran Palace to the Vatican. He had the covered passageway built, still existing today, that connects St. Peter's to Castel Sant'Angelo, creating a route that permitted many later popes to flee danger and take refuge. At the end of the Babylonian captivity, during which the papal see was located in Avignon, the various conditions imposed on the citizens of Rome before the pope would reenter the city included surrender of the castle, which thus, in 1377, finally became papal property. It was during those years, during yet another struggle for power, that the building lost its marble facing. Nicolò Lamberti, serving as the military architect for Boniface IX

The Pauline apartment, named for Paul III, was sumptuously decorated by Perino del Vaga with frescoes honoring the pope's deeds. The history of Rome and Alexander the Great are presented to exalt the pope's moral virtues in his double role of St. Paul and Alexander. Hadrian and the archangel Michael appear in the frescoes on the short walls. Among the artists who took part in works in the castle were Girolamo Siciolante (da Sermoneta), Baccio da Montelupo, Pellegrino Tibaldi, and Marco Pino.

(1389–1404), updated the building's defenses to better withstand the force of cannons. The main drum with the funerary chamber was strategically set back, surrounded by walkways built around the structure. Access to the entryway was restricted to a single sloping ramp. Prisons were built to the side of the tomb of the great Hadrian, in a sense reminding those condemned to life imprisonment of the eternity of the tomb.

The structure retained its symbolic importance. In 1453, Stefano Porcari, planning to restore Rome's republican liberty, led an antipapal revolt, and his chief aims were capturing Castel Sant'Angelo and Pope Nicholas V (1447–55). (His plot failed, and he was hanged from one of the castle's side towers.) It was under Nicholas V that the movement began to transform the fortress into a papal residence. Nicholas V had comfortable if somewhat spartan apartments built with access to the castle's courtyard. Leon Battista Alberti designed a true "curial citadel" for the popes. Under Alexander VI (1492–1503) the work was entrusted to Antonio da Sangallo the Elder, who had a deep moat dug and raised the Porta Viridaria. A new apartment, demolished in 1628, was decorated by Pinturicchio. Clement VII took refuge in the fortified site during the sack of Rome in 1527, holding out for six months against the siege, only to give in before the

powerful armies of Charles V. It was during the papacy of Clement VII that Giulio Romano decorated the walls of a hall with a magnificent frieze of putti and acanthus volutes and Giovanni da Udine decorated the private bathroom that Bramante had made for Julius II's hot me-

dicinal baths. The sixteenth-century diary of Johannes Fichard speaks of the cramped but extremely elegant room in which "His Holiness bathes in warm water poured over him by a naked young girl fashioned in bronze."

It was the next pope, Alessandro Farnese, elected pope as Paul III (1534–49), who, of all the popes, had the greatest impact on the interior decoration, planning the

BELOW: In all probability, the giant porphyry sarcophagus bearing the ashes of Hadrian originally stood in this circular room; it is located in the innermost area of the mausoleum, and for that reason was used many centuries later as the site for the treasury.

OPPOSITE: The Sala del Perseo was part of Paul III's private apartments and is named for the beautiful frieze presenting the story of Perseus made by Perino del Vaga. The wooden ceiling dates to the sixteenth century.

spectacular papal apartment on the upper floor that still bears his name (Pauline). The Farnese family coat of arms decorated the Cortile dell'Angelo, later called also the Cortile d'Onore. According to Vasari, the castellan of the castle, Tiberio Crispo, "being fond of art, wished to embellish the castle, and he rendered the loggias, rooms, and halls very beautiful for the better reception of the pope when he went there." To this end he sought the assistance of Antonio da Sangallo the Younger. The majestic Salone del Consiglio bears the Greek epigraph of the learned Alessandro Farnese, who wrote there, "Paul III, Pontifex Maximus, transformed this tomb of the deified Hadrian into a divine and regal palace." The painter Perino del Vaga (1501–1547), leading heir of the Raphael tradition, worked together with Marco Pino and Pellegrino Tibaldi in the Pauline apartments the last two years of his life, celebrating papal patronage of the arts and creating truly grandiose decoration. The Sala Regia exalted the moral virtues of its patron in the double role of St. Paul and Alexander the Great, emblematic of justice and wisdom. Hadrian and the archangel Michael were frescoed on the facing wall. Perino decorated the private rooms of the pope, the Sala di Psiche and the Sala del Perseo, open only to a few intimates, with mythological scenes from Ovid and Apuleius. A small Pompeiian

hallway decorated with grotesques led to the Sala della Biblioteca, decorated with frescoes and stuccoes by Luzio Luzzi. This room led, in turn, to a circular hall where the ashes of the deified Hadrian were preserved in a giant porphyry sarcophagus. Centuries later, this sacred

and remote area of the mausoleum served to house the Vatican treasure.

Making use of one of the great structures of antiquity, Paul III sought to sanction the ties of continuity between the ancient pagan city and the triumphant church. He did so by subjugating a monument that had witnessed struggles for power in the city from the beginning of Christianity. Under his rule, Raffaello da Montelupo was commissioned to make an angel to stand atop the castle

to replace the one destroyed in the sack of 1527 (Raffaello's statue was in turn replaced in 1753). And in gold letters he had inscribed on the ceiling of the Sala Paolina, "Everything that is within this fortress, once crumbling, inaccessible, and defaced, now, by merit of Pope Paul III, has been restored, put back in order, and decorated to create enduring strength, commodious use, and subtle elegance."

Clement VII had the private bathroom decorated with stuccoes and frescoes by Giovanni da Udine; it was probably built by Bramante for the hot medicinal baths of Julius II. In his sixteenth-century diary Johannes Fichard describes the narrow but extremely elegant room in which "His Holiness bathes in warm water poured over him by a naked young girl fashioned in bronze."

OPPOSITE: The grand hall of the library was decorated by the artists of Paolo III, with the stuccos and frescoes by Luzio Luzi illustrating marine and mythological scenes of sileni, centaurs, and sirens. The room is named after the keeper of the Vatican Archives' confidential papers.

Palazzo Spada

At the height of their power and fortune, the Capodiferro family commissioned the architect Bartolomeo Baronino to build an elegant residence for Cardinal Girolamo, the pride and glory of that ancient Roman family as well as a highly cultured man, learned and

refined, an outstanding example of the ideals of the humanistic life. Work began in 1549 and kept to such a brisk pace that the palace had been completed by the spring of 1550, in time to be inaugurated during the jubilee celebrations. The facade of the palace dates to that period and is still intact. Its decorations in stucco, fresco, and graffito work follow a style that was widespread in the first half of the sixteenth century and that had conferred on the city a sense of gaiety and artistic complexity

ABOVE: The palace still has its sixteenth-century facade animated with exuberant decoration. Finished in time for the jubilee celebrations in 1550, the building was designed by Bartolomeo Baronino, but its decoration was entrusted to teams of artists led by Giulio Mazzoni and Diego di Fiandra, Tomasso del Bosco, and Leonardo Stormani. The decorative program, based on famous figures from Roman history, is linked to that of the Branconio dell'Aquila Palace, designed by Raphael, which was destroyed in 1519.

OPPOSITE: The famous false-perspective colonnade by Francesco Borromini was made for Virgilio Spada, Cardinal Bernardino's brother.

that is now difficult to imagine. Standing over the main door is the coat of arms of the building's patron, Paul III, whose grandiose palace had recently been built nearby with the assistance of Baronino. The somewhat complicated shape of Palazzo Spada reflects an earlier structure, a corner of which was partially preserved. The courtyard and the facade were both decorated by Giulio Mazzoni, and both have niches holding antique-style figures of Olympian divinities alternating with the coats of arms of Julius II and Henry II of France. (The cardinal, described as "amiable, handsome, good-humored, and adored by all," had spent much of his life in France, serving as papal nuncio to the court of Catherine de' Medici, wife of Henry II.)

Inside the palace, the series of rooms on the *piano nobile* constitutes an impressive repertory of manneristic style. Because the pictures seem to be part of the architecture, set in stucco frames at fixed positions, the gallery has been called a "small Italian Fontainebleau." The stuccoes and frescoes by Mazzoni and his circle exalt a style of beauty bursting with references to Hellenistic art and Roman art, in particular grotesques and other motifs taken from the "antiques and curiosities" unearthed from antiquity and avidly praised some decades earlier by the students of Raphael. The playful and capriciously inventive spirit of mannerism

BELOW: Cardinal Girolamo's refined but fanciful taste is amply displayed in the Galleria degli Stucchi. These painted decorations and stuccoes by Giulio Mazzoni and his workshop present scenes from Ovid's *Metamorphoses* and ancient history, including Narcissus studying his reflection in a pool of water (opposite).

predominates throughout the rooms. It is an elegance generated by courtly pleasures that were destined to be reined in soon by the reforms of the Council of Trent. The scenes present the *Metamorphoses* of Ovid, the four parts of the world, the four seasons, and the four elements; they

The Sala delle Stagioni is completely covered with decorations by Mazzoni; at the center is the scene of *Water*, flanked by *Spring* on one side and *Autumn* on the other.

OPPOSITE: Detail of the figure of a youth, modeled by Giulio Mazzoni, that supports the stucco pilaster strip on the wall of the Sala delle Stagioni.

allude to that complex relationship of continuity between the pagan world and Christian culture to which the patron aspired. From the gallery one enters the Stanza della Ninfa Callisto, work of the workshop of Giulio Mazzoni, then pass into the Stanza di Enea and the Stanza di Achille, both tied to the artistic style of the circle of Perino del Vaga. Recent studies indicate that the frieze presenting episodes from ancient history can be ascribed to Sicciolante da Sermoneta, while the frescoes of Love

and Psyche are attributed to an artist of the circle of Pellegrino Tibaldi.

In 1632, the palace was bought by Cardinal Bernardino Spada and his brother Virgilio, and under their ownership it experienced a rebirth during the baroque period. The Spada name has come to be attached to the palace primarily because of the extraordinary collection of art they placed in it. From the moment they acquired it, Bernardino began directing

the restoration and expansion of the building, adding another wing. The studiolo was designed to accommodate Bernardino's interests in perspective, astronomy, and astrology, not to mention the poetry that, for his amusement, he composed in Latin. A special area was dedicated to housing the collection of paintings he had assembled during his stay in Bologna; this area may have begun as the cardinal's private collection, but it soon had all the

Bernardino Spada's art collection, which he began in 1630, is displayed today in a gallery on the palace's second floor. It is composed of paintings and works in sculpture, and although relatively small, it offers invaluable insight into the cardinal's taste as a collector, while at the same time testifying to the relationships he enjoyed with some of the leading artists of his period, such as Guido Reni, who made a portrait of him in 1631.

qualities of a true gallery. From 1627 to 1631, Bernardino had served as papal legate to Bologna, and he had come to know and patronize the city's leading artists. He developed a particular passion for the paintings of the Emilian region and continued adding to his collection even after his return to Rome. He was also quite fond of having his portrait painted, as can be seen in the famous portrait commissioned in 1631 of Guido Reni, with whom he began a close relationship during his stay in Bologna. We know his features also from a painting by Guercino, whom he contacted for the execution of frescoes in the royal palace of Luxembourg back during his period as papal nuncio in Paris, when he was acting in the name of the queen of France Marie de' Medici. These events had a lasting influence on his artistic interests and the works he collected; his brother Virgilio, a passionate student of architecture, played an important role in directing the construction projects in the palace.

Virgilio had been a member of Rome's Congregation of the Oratory since 1622. In the circle of his patron, Innocent X, and in particular by way of the members of the Oratory, he met Francesco Borromini. It was Borromini who designed the famous example of trompe l'oeil for Palazzo Spada. This magnificent arched colonnade is only thirty feet long but seems far

Guercino, *The Death of Dido*, 1631.

longer, its columns rapidly diminishing as they recede from the viewer: what seems to be a life-size statue at the end is, in reality, barely a foot tall. In constructing this Borromini made use of the knowledge of the Augustinian mathematician Giovanni Mario da Bitonto, replacing pictorial false perspective with an architectural false perspective that extends the restricted space into a secret garden. He displayed a similar curious bent when he made the gallery with the solar and lunar sundial, this time following the guidance of a priest of the order of the Minims of St. Francis of Paola from Trinità dei Monti.

During his time in Bologna, Bernardino Spada had become enamored of perspective views and had come into contact with the two leading perspective painters of the time, Angelo Michele Colonna (1604–1687) and Agostino Mitelli (1609–1660). He summoned both these artists to Rome to make the ornamental decoration of the so-called Sala di Pompeo, which takes its name from the colossal statue of that emperor that still dominates the room. In his *Felsina Pittrice*, a history of Bolognese painters, Carlo Cesare Malvasia records the constant meddling of the cardinal in the workyard and the equally constant complaints of the two Bolognese artists.

Now owned by the Italian state, Palazzo Spada is headquarters of the Council of State. The arched colonnade by Borromini is open to the public, as is the seventeenth-century gallery, which houses Bernardino's collection of paintings and sculpture in a suitably baroque atmosphere.

In 1632 Cardinal Spada commissioned painters, decorators, stuccoworkers, gilders, and carvers to create works for many of the palace's rooms, while also restoring them. These rooms included the great Salone di Pompeo, named for the colossal statue then thought to represent Pompey that still stands at the center. The statue had been found in 1552 and given to Cardinal Girolamo Capodiferro by Pope Julius III. Two artists from Bologna, Angelo Michele Colonna and Agostino Mitelli, were called in to make pictorial decorations, and they demonstrated their skills with perspective views.

Palazzo dei Conservatori

Since the mythic age of Romulus and Remus the Capitoline Hill has been the heart of Rome. It was on the summit of this hill that the acropolis of the Tarquins stood. Later, smaller structures too numerous to count, including altars, statues, and chapels, were erected randomly up and down the slope of the hill around the magnificent temple of Jupiter Capitolinus. Roman generals returning in glory to the great city made their way up the slope, cheered on by the thronging populace, to place offerings on altars and to perform ritual sacrifices at the feet of the temple of Saturn. The hill was damaged by fires many times in antiquity, necessitating several reconstructions. Each of these projects was followed by an even larger one, every one of them, as Cassiodorus wrote, "exceeding the capacity of human ingenuity."

Abandonment came with the fall of Rome. The temples fell into ruin one by one, the columns were broken apart and reduced to lime in kilns set up for the purpose on the plain below. The time came when even the place-names had to be changed: Monte Caprino ("goat hill")

OPPOSITE: The Palazzo dei Conservatori was reconstructed in the middle of the fifteenth century under Pope Nicholas V, who made it the residence of the conservators, elected officials charged with the administration of the city. Michelangelo began work restructuring the building's facade in 1563; Guidetto Guidetti continued the work following Michelangelo's design; and it was completed by Giacomo della Porta in 1568.

ABOVE: The large windows with balcony on the second floor are flanked by half-columns and topped by arched pediments decorated with a shell motif.

or Monte Vaccino ("cow hill") seemed far more suitable for these fields used for cattle grazing and dotted with heaps of ruins. During these truly Dark Ages the ancient Corsi family built its first fortified towers in the area; then, around the period of the first millennium, the population of Rome got back into the habit of meeting on the Capitoline, and it once again became the center of the city.

During the pontificate of Paul III (Alessandro Farnese), famous as one of the happiest in Roman history, large-scale building projects were undertaken, part of an extensive program of major urban renewal. At some point, the decision was made to radically transform the chaotic assembly of battlemented structures in this area. Paul III hoped to heal the wounds of the bloody sack of Rome in 1527, and he was beautifying the most important areas of the city with new works. The pope chose Palazzo Venezia for his summer residence; it was fortified and connected to the Capitoline Hill by means of a suspended corridor. Since the Middle Ages a great many of the citizens of Rome had been hostile to the excessive power of the church, and this had led to centuries of feuds among various factions. As an age-

In the courtyard are fragments of ancient works, such as the colossal head of Constantine, which, together with the pointing hand and several others pieces, belonged to the forty-foot-high statue of the emperor, made of marble and gilt wood, that once decorated the basilica of Constantine. Reliefs and statues, pillars and inscriptions recall the time of the Caesars.

old symbol of republican liberty, the Capitoline was one of the areas that Paul III had his eye on; he hoped to use it in his efforts to reassert papal authority in the city. A benediction loggia, later transformed in Palazzo dei Musei Capitoline, was set up to mark this papal presence. Michelangelo, summoned by Farnese, returned to Rome in 1534 to plan these projects, which were destined to keep him occupied on and off until the end of his life. The transformation of this zone began in the first days of 1538 with the transfer of the monumental bronze equestrian statue of Emperor Marcus Aurelius from its original position near St. John Lateran to the center of Piazza Campidoglio. Years were to pass before, in 1562, Michelangelo finally undertook construction of the facade of the Palazzo dei Conservatori, opposite which he decided to put a twin structure, the Palazzo Nuovo; the reworked Palazzo Senatorio marked off the third side of the piazza, the city spreading behind it; and a balustrade ran along the fourth side, its opening flanked by the Dioscuri.

Michelangelo died before completing this project. Those who followed him remained faithful to his instructions, at least in terms of the general layout. He was replaced by one of his pupils, Giacomo della Porta, who, except for a few modifications, followed the directives of the great master. By the end of 1580, the facade of the

Palazzo dei Conservatori had been finally completed.

The original palace, built during the fifteenth century at the request of Nicholas V, had not been demolished but simply restored and updated in accordance with contemporary canons. The portico had been used as the setting

A portico at the end of the courtyard protects the colossal statue of *Rome*, made during the period of Trajan.

for the first sculptures of the Capitoline collection, founded by Sixtus IV in 1471 (considered the first public museum of classical sculpture since antiquity), including statues of river divinities, the She-Wolf, emblem of the city, and the *Spinario*. The city's ancient guilds had their headquarters on the ground floor: the apothecaries and innkeepers, craftsmen and carpenters met under the arches to discuss their rights. The secular power of the conservators and the senators who had for so many years administered justice on this spot was slowly being drained of all meaning. The city's sense of independence, the roots of which grew directly from the soil of the Capitoline Hill, was being eroded, replaced by the absolute rule of the church. The halls on the *piano nobile*, frescoed in the fifteenth and sixteenth centuries by such artists as Jacopo Ripando with the stories of ancient Rome, were reached by way of an austere, monumental stairway designed by Michelangelo. Several rooms were decorated during the first half of the 1540s. The friezes of the salas called delle Aquile or delle Oche present scenes of Roman history alternating with views of ancient and modern Rome. The friezes in the Sala del Trono, dated 1544, represent episodes of the life of Scipio mixed with statuary groups. The creator

In the Salone degli Orazi e dei Curiazi, the Cavaliere d'Arpino painted episodes from the birth of Rome, with battles between Horatii and Curiatii, the rape of the Sabine women, and the battle between Romans and the men of Veii and Fidenae. At the two ends of the room, Gian Lorenzo Bernini and Alessandro Algardi placed, respectively, the marble statue of Urban VII and the great bronze of Innocent X.

of these frescoes was a student of Salviati, the Spaniard Pedro de Rubiales. The great Sala degli Orazi e dei Curiazi, decorated by Giuseppe Cesari, the artist best known as Cavaliere d'Arpino (1568–1640), presented a series of *Histories of Ancient Rome.* The commission, given to him as a "unique painter, rare and excellent," kept him busy the rest of his life. Documents indicate that he made the first fresco of the great epic cycle between January and May 1596. This was *The Discovery of Romulus and Remus,* taken from Livy's *History of Rome.* Records of payments made the next year refer to the execution of the famous *Battle between Romans and the Men of Veii and Fidenae,* an outstanding example of the late sixteenth-century painting style that showed a marked preference for clarity and symmetry, harmony and a classical sense. The highly admired and powerful Cavaliere was kept busy in the Conservatori for all of thirty years. In 1612 he painted the *Fight between the Horatii and the Curiatii,* a history painting par excellence, which directed the Roman school of painting toward figurative constructions that were legible and clear but also grandiose in their intentions. All work was then suspended until 1630, despite the repeated warnings from the sponsors. In the seventeenth century, Bernini and Alessandro Algardi set the two gigantic statues of their benefactors, Urban VIII and Innocent X, at the sides

Jacopo Ripanda and workshop, *Hannibal on an Elephant,* c. 1610.

of the great hall to replace the earlier statue of Sixtus V, which had been destroyed.

Miraculously spared damage during the many and various periods of destruction during our times, the Piazza Campidoglio and the Palazzo dei Conservatori remain emblematic of the history of Rome. The buildings on the piazza designed by Michelangelo are today the headquarters of the city's picture collection and archaeological collection, including the original statue of Marcus Aurelius; the version in the piazza, standing on a base designed by Michelangelo, is a copy.

The Sala dei Trionfi is decorated by a frieze by Michele Alberti and Giacomo Rocchetti depicting the triumph of Aemilius Paullus over Perseus of Macedon, from 1569. In the center is the famous Roman bronze called the *Spinario*, based on a model from the Hellenistic age.

OPPOSITE: The *Venere Esquilina*, found in the villa Palombara and done in marble, is an example of Roman statuary from the first century and is modeled after the Greek sculpture by Paraxiteles.

Palazzo Sacchetti

For almost twenty years, Antonio da Sangallo the Younger (1484–1546) reigned uncontested in Rome as the favorite architect of the rising aristocracy, for whomw he designed substantial homes that may reflect his early career as a military architect. The palace was his central theme, and he meditated tirelessly on its possible permutations. A student of Bramante, Sangallo had lived through the birth of the humanistic ideals only to witness their slow transformation over the century into formal, academic concepts. Michelangelo held him partly responsible for the loss of what he called "sweet intellectual freedom," blaming him for giving in to the new Tridentine reforms that in many ways brought an end to a generation of experimental artists.

Antonio da Sangallo designed Palazzo Sacchetti in Via Giulia for himself and his family, as indicated by a plaque to the left of the balcony: "Domus. Antonii. Sangalli. Architecti MDXLIII." Sangallo already owned two buildings on this street when, in 1542, he was given a new site on which to build by the Vatican Chapter, a site

The palace, inhabited first by Antonio da Sangallo, then by Cardinal Giovanni Ricci, and followed by the Ceuli family, stands near the Tiber River, from which it is separated by a walled garden. The loggia at the far end of the garden was built by the Ceuli family of Pisan bankers. Being Tuscan, they frequented the nearby Tuscan community centered on the Church of San Giovanni de' Fiorentini.

protected from the terrible floods of the Tiber. A famous artist, the favorite of the powerful, Sangallo had the financial means to build a magnificent home, but this dream was denied him by fate. When he died in 1546, work on the palace had only just begun. The amount of work completed following Sangallo's death and the true rate of its progress are difficult to assess, not only because of vagueness in the relevant documents but because the building's next owner made substantial alterations.

The new owner was Cardinal Giovanni Ricci of Montepulciano, a powerful member of the Tuscan community that met in the nearby Church of San Giovanni dei Fiorentini (which experienced its own troubled periods). The cardinal bought the palace in Via Giulia from the architect's son Orazio in 1552. He then set about having it enlarged and altered to suit the needs of a cardinal's court. New rooms were planned following the acquisition of the adjacent house owned by the Massari brothers of Narni. The work of enlarging the palace was entrusted to Nanni di Baccio Bigio, a follower of the Sangallo tradition. Indeed, he interpreted that master's spirit perfectly, bringing the work to completion with a notable display of technical skill. He became the cardinal's favorite architect, entrusted with the cardinal's apartments in the Vatican as well as the remodeling of his

Some of the sixteenth-century rooms on the *piano nobile*, built at the time of Sangallo, were decorated with stuccowork and frescoes by the French artist Jacquiot Ponce, who worked for the powerful Cardinal Ricci. The Stanza di Alessandro presents episodes from the life of Alexander the Great, arranged following a sixteenth-century cadence.

villa outside the city, which was to house his extraordinary collection (known today as Villa Medici because of later owners). Nanni followed most of Sangallo's plans for the ground floor, but in the overall sense he created a new building. Following Nanni's death, Giacomo della Porta took over direction of the work and made some slight changes. The young Domenico Fontana was employed on the building site as a stucco worker.

In 1553, when the work was completed, Francesco Salviati, another Tuscan, was called to fresco the central hall, known as the Salone del Mappamondo. He created an extraordinary decorative cycle, a display of experimental fantasy, a work of playful exuberance and ingenuity. The Old Testament stories of David and Bathsheba are arranged on the basis of pure artifice, as paintings within paintings or paintings on top of other paintings. Like all the other great artists of his generation, those who brought the adroit beauty of mannerism to its greatest heights, Salviati opened his works onto new vistas, far removed from the naturalness, symmetry, and harmony of the Renaissance. Amid fantastic painted frames of festoons and garlands, nude figures, truly painted sculptures, collapse languidly over the tops of doors draped with cloths. With their astonishing spatial organization, these frescoes represent one of the most fascinating creations of

The Ceuli family amassed a large collection of ancient marbles and sculptures, and these pieces were displayed in the palace until they were bought by Scipione Borghese.

OPPOSITE: The splendid carved ceiling dates to the period when the palace was owned by the banker Tiberio Ceuli, who bought it from Giulio Ricci in 1576, and set about embellishing it. The coat of arms at the center is that of the Sacchetti family, who became owners of the palace in 1642 after moving to Rome following disagreements with the Medici family.

sixteenth-century painting. With the cardinal's death in 1576, ownership of the palace passed to the Ceuli, a family of Pisan bankers who had moved to Rome. They saw to the completion its decoration and used it to house a collection of antique sculpture; 273 marble works were inventoried there before being transferred to the Vatican Museum. Tiberio Ceuli also commissioned the creation of the gallery, with a magnificent ceiling frescoed with prophets and sibyls by Giacomo Rocca, a painter who emulated Michelangelo and owned a collection of drawings by that master. The grotto, with its rustic mosaics, also dates to this period. The Ceuli family's heraldic motif with stars appears in the five rooms off the garden. The layout of the building was considerably altered with the addition of two new wings and a loggia facing the river and overlooking the garden.

In 1608 the palace became the property of Cardinal Ottavio Aquaviva of Aragon, who had a private chapel built.

Since 1649 the palace has been home to the Sacchetti family, who moved from Fiesole, above Florence, to what, all those many years later, was still the Tuscan quarter of Rome. Under these new owners the palace experienced a true rebirth. The brothers Marcello and Giulio, the latter a cardinal, distinguished themselves during the seventeenth century for their great classical learning

Ricci built the gallery in 1573, but its decoration was completed during its later ownership by the Ceuli family, who commissioned Giacomo Rocca to decorate the walls with sibyls and prophets. Rocca took his inspiration from models by Michelangelo, for whom he nourished profound admiration, as indicated by the many studies he made of Michelangelo's works.

and as leading patrons of the arts. Their home became a center of refined patronage as the two brothers carefully created a splendid picture collection. Word spread that no more than the cardinal's shadow was needed to ensure a painter's success. They were the principal supporters of that great master of decoration, Pietro da Cortona, who painted a magnificent portrait of Cardinal Giulio. The dome and the lantern at the center of the private chapel were certainly conceived early in Pietro's career and were decorated by Agostino Ciampelli. In the dining room overlooking the Tiber, in the wing that had been built by the banker Ceuli, he made two frescoes, *Adam and Eve* and *The Holy Family*, but he concentrated his efforts on the extraordinary villa in the Pineta Sacchetti, today sadly destroyed. In 1660, Carlo Rainaldi was called in to change the grotto, which he had flanked by a wall along the Tiber side where people could play boccie. The loggias were closed in halfway through the nineteenth century, but the part of the building overlooking the river, built on a design by Giovan Battista Contini, has been standing since 1699.

The famous collection of paintings assembled by Marcello and Giulio Sacchetti during the seventeenth century was sold by the marchese Giovanni Battista in 1748 to Pope Benedict XIV. The pope put the paintings together with the collection

The Salone dei Mappamondi on the *piano nobile,* with frescoes by Francesco Salviati, is named for the two globes in the room, bu it is best known for the paintings that Salviati made between 1553 and 1554 for Cardinal Ricci of Montepulciano, who chose the theme himself: the story of King David.

of Cardinal Pio and used them as the basis for the creation of the Pinacoteca Capitolina, the first public museum in history. In the spring of 1991 the palace was used as the setting for an exhibition dedicated to Roman art. What better site than Salviati's magnificently eccentric vault to evoke the golden age of the city's artistic patronage?

Francesco Salviati, from the stories of King David, David dancing in front of the ark, and a detail of the frescoes.

Palazzo Pecci Blunt

This palace, with its simple and elegant facade facing the Michelangelo stairway in the Campidoglio, was built in the first half of the sixteenth century for the Albertoni family, unrivaled rulers of this quarter. Of ancient Roman origin, the family was well known for their venerated ancestor Ludovica, immortalized in Bernini's sculpture *Blessed Ludovica Albertoni*, for the Church of San Francesco at Ripa. Cardinals and administrators, the Paluzzi Albertoni lived in their quarter, building other homes on the Campitelli and Margana piazzas.

Around 1550, the palace on Piazza dell'Aracoeli was acquired by Cardinal Silvestro Gottardi. Soon after, it was bought by Maria Fani; the Fani family had the palace restructured by Giacomo della Porta (1532–1602), who lived in the palace during the last years of the sixteenth century and later bought an adjacent building. Several decades later the palace passed to the Marchese Bartolomeo Ruspoli, who lived there before moving to his home on the Via del Corso—it was, in fact, the first Roman residence of the Ruspoli family, originally

LEFT: The simple, elegant facade of the sixteenth-century palace, built for the Albertoni family, stands opposite the Campidoglio stairs designed by Michelangelo. It was originally composed of two floors topped by an elaborate cornice, but a third floor and a roof terrace were added during the nineteenth century. The large central door has a linear architrave, a motif repeated in the windows along the second floor.

OPPOSITE: The decorations in the main dining room on the *piano nobile* include this statue of Venus.

from Tuscany. Meanwhile various illustrious prelates had lived in the palace, including Cardinal Federico Borromeo, Cardinal Sfrondati, and Bernardino Spada. Early in the seventeenth century the building became the home of the Malatesta counts, and in 1929 it became the property of the Pecci Blunt family, its current owners.

The palace originally had two floors topped by an elegant cornice; the linear architraves of the windows on the second floor repeat the motif of the main door. A roof terrace added during the nineteenth century gives the palace a panoramic view. Rusticated stonework runs along the entire length of the building on the outside corners. The jewel of this construction was the stuccoed loggia with its wealth of frescoes and gilding; it was commissioned in the middle of the sixteenth century by the Genoese Cardinal Serra. This residence, conferred on him by the Pontifical State, was connected to Via di Tor de'

Specchi by way of the garden. Students of the Zuccaro brothers worked in the vast apartments of the *piano nobile*, including Ventura Salimbeni and Gaspard Dughet. Paintings have been found on ceiling panels of a small loggia in the palace; once attributed to Dughet, they are now attributed to a student of that artist. These represent the creation of Eve, Lot leaving Sodom, the daughters of Lot, Balaam and the angel, Abraham and Hagar, Hagar and Ishmael in the desert, and

The frieze along the walls of the main parlor was done by a painter of the Zuccaro school in a late-mannerist style, and dates to the sixteenth century. The vine-motif decoration on the beams running across the parlor's coffered ceiling was probably made during the seventeenth century when the palace was owned by the Ruspoli family.

Tobias and the fish. Marie Nicole Boisclair, author of a work on Gaspard Dughet, is inclined to attribute this delightful decorative cycle with its dense landscapes to the painter Pier Francesco Mola. In his work on seventeenth-century Roman landscape paintings Luigi Salerno also refutes the attribution of these works to Dughet. Ventura Salimbeni was probably the primary artist of one cycle of frescoes. This Siena-born artist had been in Rome since at least 1585 (at which time he is recorded as a witness at a trial) to paint in the Lateran palace in the benediction loggia and in the Sistine Library at the side of

Cesare Nebbia and Giovanni Guerra. In the frescoes in Palazzo Pecci Blunt he displays, aside from a festive and joyous spirit, the storytelling skills, vivacious and spontaneous, that later won him important commissions, such as the decorations of Santa Maria Maggiore, the Church of the Gesù, and the facade of Palazzo Verospi. The great popularity he enjoyed was due most of all to the technical and narrative skills he first displayed in these frescoes. Giovanni Baglione, whose *Vite* ("Lives") takes up where Vasari left off, described him as restless, superficial, and little interested in his studies. The short biog-

raphy ends, "But to tell the truth, while he inspired great hopes for himself in his professors, who thought great things were sure to come from him when they saw his early works, for he showed such great spirit and technical skills, he later became lazy and sluggish; and spent all his time with his paramours; and thus he never achieved the great things that had been hoped for from him." Even so, there is that elegant sophistication in forms and also the clear and vibrant colors that we find in the frieze in the room on the *piano nobile*.

The frescoes by Federico and Taddeo Zuccaro and

A series of rooms leads to the small, covered loggia decorated with landscapes by a student of Dughet. The paintings present the creation of Eve, Lot leaving Sodom, the daughters of Lot, Balaam and the angel, Abraham and Hagar, Hagar and Ishmael in the desert, and Tobias and the fish. At the center of the room, a Roman alabaster vase stands on a short column. The vault (following pages) is covered with sixteenth-century stuccoes.

their assistants reflect the dictates of the manneristic style of painting, the leading exponent of which in Rome had been Perino del Vaga. The elongated, sinuous figures move within increasingly complex and cerebral settings. The chromatic range is broad, but the vision is principally projected on surfaces. The themes chosen are allusions to ancient mythology or events in the Old Testament. The Sala degli Arazzi still has Flemish tapestries hung on its walls. From the entry one passes through a small private chapel. On the walls are four paintings of the evangelists by Lucas van Leyden and a series of works by the Genoese artist Stefano Magnasco, and the heraldic emblem of vine leaves is repeated in the painted beams of the coffered ceiling. The coat of arms of the Malatesta family appears on each of the four corners of the frieze in the next room.

The Pecci Blunt family, current owners of the palace, have restored the gallery on the ground floor using marbles from the famous Medici company, the same company that earlier restored the *piano nobile.*

The palace has a small family chapel located amid sumptuously decorated sixteenth-century rooms that have been restored with great care by the palace's current owners, the Pecci Blunt.

Palaces from Baroque
to Neoclassicism

Palazzo Doria Pamphili, Galleria
degli Specchi.

Palazzo Ruspoli Rucellai

This enormous structure with its severe features faces Via del Corso, once known as Via Lata, the main avenue that had been the center of the city since the seventeenth century, thus enjoying the role that had belonged in antiquity to the Campus Martius when the emperor Augustus had decided to build his mausoleum on that site. Many Roman families had built their palaces along this avenue, amid the remains of the Ara Pacis (Altar of Peace) and the Arco di Portogallo (demolished during the reign of Pope Alexander VII). During the Carnival celebrations on the eve of Lent the balconies and facades of buildings along the avenue were elaborately decorated.

An early structure had been built by the family of the Jacobilli, who had moved to Rome from Foligno to carry on their careers as city administrators. Little remains of that ancient structure, however, for it was entirely reworked in 1583, on the initiative of Orazio Rucellai, by Bartlomeo Ammanati, "his great friend," as Baglione recorded in his *Vite* ("Lives"). Orazio was a refined Florentine gentleman, lover of

LEFT: The austere facade of the original palace built by the Jacobilli family was completed for Orazio Rucellai, who came into possession of the building in 1583, by the architect Bartolomeo Ammanati. At that time, the nineteen windows opening on the Via del Corso were added, each supported by decorative corbels.

OPPOSITE: The grand staircase was made by Martino Longhi II for the Caetani family, later owners of the great palace. From its completion, it was extolled by seventeenth-century chroniclers, who listed it among the wonders of Rome. The loggia of the *piano nobile*, also designed by Martino Longhi II, originally had no windows. It is decorated by sculptures from the classical period set in niches.

literature, in particular the verses of Torquato Tasso. According to the reports left us by an anonymous chronicle of the period, he was a "youth gifted with great prudence, singular virtues, sharp genius, and pleasing aspect." Although the attribution to Ammanati is given consistently in old guidebooks, it has been the subject of debate among scholars. A man of immense wealth, Orazio Rucellai was able to make his Roman home glitter, and although he was involved in intense diplomatic activity at the French court that took him out of the city for long periods, he was able to fill the halls of his home with an impressive collection of antique sculpture. He also saw to the decoration of a large gallery on the *piano nobile* by Jacopo Zucchi, an exuberant Tuscan painter then much in vogue in the circle of eclectic lovers of antiquity. In 1586, Zucchi completely covered the walls with allegorical figures, following the complex late-mannerist iconography that glorified the genealogy of the gods and the triumphs of the kings of Rome, in keeping with the tradition, by then widely embraced, of

covering the walls of palaces with scenes based on some scholarly, literary theme. He was an artist of broad learning, quite familiar with Horace's maxim (from his *Ars Poetics*) *"Ut pictura poesis"* ("as is painting, so is poetry"), according to which painting should echo verse and follow similar harmonies. The painter had trained in the studio of Vasari, and his style had been forged in the Florentine studiolo of Ferdinando de' Medici in Palazzo Vecchio, in which animals and plants, crystals, images from the arts and crafts of mankind, had been blended in

alchemical references with hermetic meanings. On the walls of Palazzo Rucellai, Jacopo Zucchi presented what amounts to a catalog of erudite interests during the late sixteenth century, a cosmological presentation of encyclopedic breadth.

With Orazio's death, in 1605, the splendid palace became the property of his sons Luigi and then Ferdinando. Since Ferdinando was without heirs, he transferred it to Luigi Caetani, in 1629, for the price of 51,000 florins. Under the guidance of Bartolomeo Breccioli, a family architect, extensive renova-

tions were undertaken. A student of Fontana and connoisseur of mathematics and hydraulics, Breccioli directed various improvements in the cornice and the mezzanines, designing the facade on Via dei Fontanella Boghese. The cardinal had Martino Longhi II erect a "comfortable, charming, and luminous" staircase entirely covered with slabs of Parian marble. Statues were set in niches. It earned praise as one of "the most beautiful stairways in Rome, with all the requisites called for in a magnificent palace." Despite the large-scale reworking of the

ABOVE: On the wall with windows, Jacopo Zucchi painted the heads of the Roman emperors; above each are the vices and virtues associated with him.

OPPOSITE: Orazio Rucellai commissioned Jacopo Zucchi to make the gallery. He wanted Zucchi to paint a large mythological epic depicting the genealogy of the Gods. This attempt to revive the style of the antique became one of the principle decorative cycles of the late sixteenth century in Rome.

apartments in the 1630s and 1640s and the new layout given the palace, the members of the Caetani family spent little time in their home on the Corso, preferring their holdings in Sermoneta. Their heavy debts, combined with the gradual erosion of their political influence, must certainly have influenced their decision to sell the property, in 1713, to the Ruspoli family, who already had their family chapel in the nearby church of San Lorenzo in Lucina.

The Ruspoli family's long stay proved to be an exciting period for the palace, which became the setting for many memorable celebrations and events. It was Francesco Maria Marescotti Ruspoli, a poet in his own right, who created all this great cultural excitement and organized the literary entertainments that took place in the palace during the second half of the eighteenth century. He brought a lively and extroverted spirit to the salons, which proved well suited to the new life being led there. Theatrical performances were held in the Salone delle Accademia similar to those that Cardinal Pietro Ottoboni arranged in the Cancelleria, but it was music more than anything else that reached levels of exquisite quality under the prince's guidance. During one series of celebrations he directed the construction of a highly ornate temporary loggia on which the musicians took their places. George Frideric

BELOW: At the center of the great allegorical ceiling, Jacopo Zucchi presented Apollo in his chariot drawn by four winged horses; to his side are the Hours and Aurora; the episode to the left, with the god of war, Mars, is an allusion to violence and discord, while to the right is the fable of the birth of Venus, who rises from the waves on sea foam.

OPPOSITE: This image from Jacopo Zucchi's paintings on the vault of the ceiling shows the allegorical chariot of the Moon in her three forms—as Luna in the sky, Diana on the earth, and Hecate in the underworld. In her hands she holds the key to those regions, and she is accompanied by a deer and by Dew.

Handel, Arcangelo Corelli, and Alessandro Scarlatti often met in the halls on the *piano nobile.* Austerity having fallen out of fashion, the rooms on the ground floor were decorated with an extraordinary variety of colorful decorative cycles. Views of the family's estates were followed by playful works by Antonio Amorosi, who painted scenes of popular celebrations during country outings, at which times the villas were thrown open to peasants. Hunting scenes and scenes with soldiers, seascapes and hillside views enlivened the walls and kept busy a team of more than thirty painters, including Alessio de Marchesi, Johann Paul Schor, Onofrio Loth, Michelangelo Cerruti, and Andrea Locatelli. These decorations were destroyed in the nineteenth century when, in keeping with a trend then sweeping across all Europe, the ground floor of the building was transformed into a restaurant, in this case the famous Caffé Nuovo.

Many of the famous guests who stayed in the rooms of Palazzo Ruspoli, from the duke of Nevers to Cardinal Borgia, whiled away time trying to decipher the mysterious harmony of the gallery's painted vault. In 1830, the palace was visited by the former queen of Holland Hortense de Beauharnais, who arrived with her son, the future Napoleon III.

In the elegant salon furnished with seventeenth-century furniture is *Marina*, attributed to Salvator Rosa, and mentioned in 1708 in the Ruspoli collection.

The Quirinal

Casting about for somewhere that might offer him relief from the oppressive heat of the Roman summer, Pope Gregory XIII (1572–85) asked his friend Ippolito d'Este, cardinal from Ferrara, for his land up on the Quirinal, the highest of Rome's seven hills. Ippolito gave it to him willingly since he himself was directing all his energies southward, to Tivoli. The summer heat and humidity in Rome drove popes—and cardinals—to flee the Vatican, which was believed to be a particularly poor location during the warm months because of its proximity to the river and all that stagnant water. The Vatican, in the words of one critic, was "low, hot, and hardly healthful."

During the so-called Babylonian captivity (1309–78) the popes had lived in Avignon. Following their return to Rome, they had found the Lateran palaces in a state of deterioration and were forced to seek shelter in the St. Mark's and Ara Coeli palaces. The decision was finally made to build a new residence on the top of the Quirinal Hill in the area that was known as Monte Cavallo because of the two sculptural

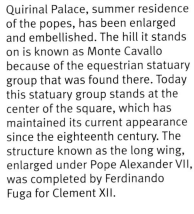

Over more than four centuries the Quirinal Palace, summer residence of the popes, has been enlarged and embellished. The hill it stands on is known as Monte Cavallo because of the equestrian statuary group that was found there. Today this statuary group stands at the center of the square, which has maintained its current appearance since the eighteenth century. The structure known as the long wing, enlarged under Pope Alexander VII, was completed by Ferdinando Fuga for Clement XII.

groups of the Dioscuri with their horses that had been found there. That residence, today known as the Quirinal, has been a close participant in the history of Rome and the Italian nation, for the Renaissance palace has gone from being the summer home of the popes to being the primary residence of the kings of Italy to being the home of Italy's president.

So many popes have had work done to enlarge or embellish this summer residence that over time the palace has

become one of the most complex in existence simply because of the length of time it, or at least some corner of it, has been under construction and the number of artists who have contributed to it. The most celebrated artists of each period have been called upon to work on the palace, and each has done so using, of course, his period's prevailing style. The industrious Gregory XIII (the same Gregory responsible for the Gregorian calendar) began the process by calling on

Ottaviano Mascherino to build the first palace, and Mascherino must have gone at this project with true fury, since the pope was able to occupy part of the building only two years after work began. The structure Mascherino built between 1583 and 1585 today constitutes the left wing of the palace, with the facade with loggia that forms one of the shorter side fronts giving onto the grand courtyard. Mascherino also designed the magnificent oval spiral staircase with coupled

columns that connects the first and second floors.

No sooner had Gregory XIII begun this work than he died; he was succeeded by one of the most extraordinary characters in papal history, Sixtus V (1585–90), another passionate builder, who immediately embraced and expanded the designs for the Quirinal, making it part of his far larger schemes that involved changes to the urban development of the city itself, from the bend in the Tiber to the hills above. This alteration was achieved by opening a series of new streets running back and forth between the major basilicas. Sixtus V had only five years as pope, but in that short time he managed to revolutionize the appearance of the city. His chief architect was Domenico Fontana, responsible for the initial arrangement of the Piazza of the Quirinal with the statuary group of the two Dioscuri that had once embellished the baths of Constantine. Fontana began work on the new palazzo on Monte Cavallo that faced onto the piazza and provided the entire city quarter with water from the aqueduct of Septimius Severus, which came to be known as the Acqua Felice. At this time the small building made by Mascherino was connected to the new palace by way of a long, low structure that was used at first to house the Swiss Guards but was destined for further changes under the pontificate of

Paul V. Sixtus V, who died in the palace on August 27, 1590, was followed by a series of lesser popes who did little to the city and the Quirinal except carry on or complete works already in progress. Clement VIII (1592–1605) directed most of his energies to the garden,

The chapel of the Annunciation, made for Paul V's private devotions, had decorations made in 1609 by Guido Reni, with assistance from Giovanni Lanfranco, Antonio Carracci, and Francesco Albani. The image at the center of the dome of the Eternal Father, set in golden angelic glories, was made by Giovanni Lanfranco.

OPPOSITE: The fresco of *Christ in Glory* by Melozzo da Forli was painted for the apse of the Church of the Holy Apostles. Clemente XI brought the painting to the Quirinal because of the deteriorating conditions in the church and installed it at the second floor of the staircase, on the wall facing the courtyard.

having several fountains put in place along with a nymphaeum and an oval pond. In 1605 one of the popes most affected by the "building disease" came to the throne, Paul V (1605–21). He showed enormous interest in the Quirinal summer residence, giving it for the first time a more official appearance. No sooner had he been made pope than he decided to finally finish the building, commissioning Flaminio Ponzio to integrate the structures made by Mascherino and Fontana, to build the datary (the office in charge of registering and dating bulls, overseeing the payment of duties, and other official tasks), and to ready a new series of rooms for decoration. At Ponzio's death in

1613, Carlo Maderno was put in charge of the worksite, and he contributed to several projects, including the planning of the two large sides, extending the building along the road that at that time led to Porta Pia. He finished the pretty rectangular courtyard and designed the chapel of the Annunciation, frescoed by Guido Reni, for the private devotions of his patron. Maderno also built the elaborate portal communicating between the chapel and the Sala Regia, topped by two angels by Pietro Bernini and a high-relief by Taddeo Landini, showing *Christ Washing the Feet of the Disciples*. Martino Ferabosco made the gilded stucco decoration on the vault. Agostino Tassi designed the frieze in the Sala

Regia about 1610 using a style that reflects the growing popularity of illusionistic perspectives among the Roman aristocracy. Agostino excelled in that style, anticipating the birth of landscape as an autonomous genre. The Sala del Concistoro, as Giovanni Baglione wrote in his *Vite* ("Lives"), was the palace's largest room and had a vaulted ceiling. It was highly admired by contemporaries; its decoration involved contributions from Orazio Gentileschi, Carlo Saraceni, and Giovanni Lanfranco, who surrounded the works by Tassi with lively, colorful figures in Oriental styles looking out of loggias over an evocative and playful perspective.

Whereas Paul V made the Quirinal into a sort of second

ABOVE: The Sala Regia, today known as the Sala dei Corazzieri, was built following a design by Maderno and is two stories high. Several artists were involved in its decoration, including Agostino Tassi, Giovanni Lanfranco, Carlo Saraceni, Giovanni Antonio Galli (known as Lo Spadarino), and Alessandro Turchi. The vault is covered with inlaid work by Giovanni Battista Soria. Located on the short wall shown here is a bas-relief of *Christ Washing the Feet of the Disciples* by Taddeo Landini, made in 1578 for a chapel in St. Peter's and brought to the Quirinal by Paul V.

OPPOSITE: In 1616 Paul V commissioned Agostino Tassi to decorate the upper frieze with false-perspective loggias from which exotic ambassadors from various nations, including this Armenian delegation, look down.

Vatican, Urban VIII (1623–44), a pragmatic man more keenly aware of the myriad dangers lurking in the world, wanted to turn it into a fortress. To render the palace nothing less than impregnable, he had it surrounded by ramparts and had high walls thrown up all around the garden. This pope, given to perusing military textbooks, proved himself to be a truly "worldly" prince, concerned first and foremost with questions of security. It was under his rule that the last remains of the grandiose baths of Constantine, until then visible in the Colonna garden, were demolished. Gianlorenzo Bernini, official architect of the pope and his family, designed the benediction loggia above the portal, where Urban appeared to dispense blessings.

Plagued by poor health, Innocent X (1644–55) retired to the Quirinal even during the winter months and undertook no large-scale alterations to the structure. Work began again, and with energy, under his successor, Alexander VII (1655–57), during whose short papacy the arts experienced an exceptional flourishing. A learned man, dignified and polite, he commissioned an astonishing number of renovations. The leader in this was Bernini, who planned a new series of halls for the Quirinal. It was during these years that the structure housing the Swiss Guards was remodeled and raised one floor higher. As recorded

by the prelate and art historian Filippo Titi, the uses of the internal spaces were changed to meet the court's changing needs. From 1657 on, leading artists working in a vareity of styles could be found side by side in the gallery of Alexander VII in a fascinating sort of artistic

competition. The leader in this effort was Pietro da Cortona, far and away the artist who best expressed the new baroque style. The resulting succession of images from this golden age presents scenes from the Old Testament. Among the artists who came to work here were Cortona's students Lazzaro Baldi and Ciro Ferri, the fol-

lowers of the Carracci style Pier Francesco Mola and Giovanni Francesco Grimaldi, along with Guglielmo Cortese, Salvator Rosa, and the landscapist Gaspard Dughet. Because of its size and the great number of artists required, Alexander VII's gallery came to be a proving

ground for artists, wisely orchestrated by the Tuscan master Pietro da Cortona. Following Pietro's death, Carlo Maratta became the outstanding painter in the city. He was a leading exponent of the classical style that culminated in the fresco of the Nativity.

Alexander VII's successors took up permanent residence

The decoration of the Sala di Ercole has been altered several times as a result of changes in the use of the room. It was originally designed as a papal apartment, but later it was among the rooms reworked by Raffaele Stern to host Napoleon between 1811 and 1812. The room was last altered in 1940, when it was made into a display room for precious tapestries.

on Monte Cavallo and set to work refining its decoration. Comfortable apartments for the papal family were built along Via Pia, and the ground floor was remodeled to house the Swiss Guards. During the eighteenth century, the Piazza del Quirinal took the appearance it has today: the obelisk was set in place above the fountain, and Innocent XIII (1721–24) commissioned Alessandro Specchi to design the stables. These, along with the annex of living quarters for the coachmen, were built alongside the Colonna garden in the area of the famous Tower of Nero, after its base, as one chronicler reported, had been "smashed away by hammerblows and mines." Clement XII (1730–40), accompanied by a retinue of two cardinals, retired to the Quirinal immediately after his coronation as pope, "for the good of the curia and the people," and lived there until his death. He commissioned Ferdinando Fuga (1699–1782) to build the "long wing" of the palace of the Consulta that faces the Quirinal, and had the famous Palazzina built on the site of several modest little houses and a corner of the garden. This jewel was designed to hold the coding office; following a northern European style, Benedict XIV (1740–58) asked Fuga to design a coffee house, as such structures were known, one that would "unite the benefits of good air with private audiences."

During the eighteenth century, a period in which learned conversations and worldly frivolities triumphed, the minor architecture of the garden experienced its moment of greatest splendor. The Palazzino di Ritiro, as it came to be known, was Fuga's final work and was decorated with landscape scenes by Jan Frans van Bloemen, known as Orizzonte, and Pompeo Batoni. As the French magistrate and writer Charles de Brosses (1709–1777) noted in his wonderful *Lettres d'Italie*, the Vatican was deserted in the eighteenth century. To Benedict XIV, the residence on the Quirinal seemed far more pleasant and comfortable; he went to St. Peter's only on the night of Corpus Domini, the nights of Holy Thursday and Saturday, and the eve of the feast of St. Peter.

Napoleon was scheduled to visit in 1812, and the preparations for this event involved further reworking of the halls of the Quirinal Palace. Imperial apartments were readied, and a team of neoclassical artists was assembled. The artists to emerge from this group include Bertel Thorvaldsen and Felice Giani, Vincenzo Pacetti and Jean-Auguste-Dominique Ingres. In the event, the French emperor never made the visit, but the rooms made ready are still intact, as are the fiery decorations made by Giani.

Having served as the official summer residence of the popes from 1592 on, the

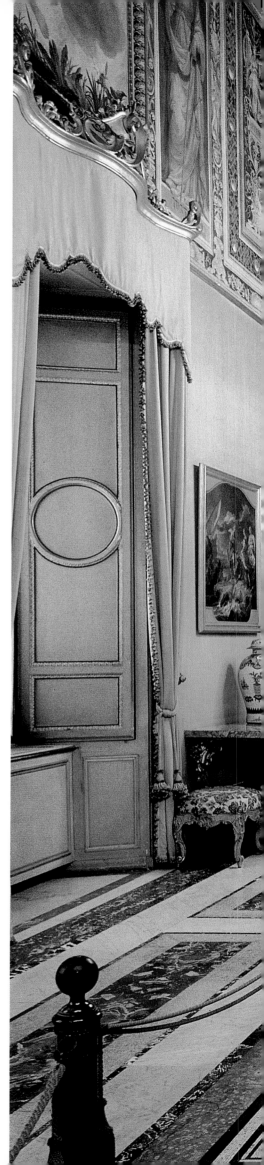

OPPOSITE: Foreign heads of state who are guests of the Quirinal are presented to the diplomatic corps in a ceremony held in the Sala degli Ambasciatori. A Roman mosaic from Hadrian's Villa is set in the center of the floor. The room was part of the complex of the famous gallery of Alexander VII, decorated by Pietro da Cortona and his students, but it was greatly altered during the nineteenth century.

Quirinal Palace began a new chapter with the decline in ecclesiastical pomp that began in 1870 with the birth of the Kingdom of Italy. New ballrooms, many of them reflecting questionable nineteenth-century taste, were built, often replacing antique decorations. Since 1947 the palace has been the residence of the president of the Italian republic.

· The four hundred years that have passed since Gregory XIII first sought to escape the heat have been full of extraordinary events, and the complex layout and decorations of this building stand as far and away the best testimony to that long span of time.

The Sala del Trono, also known as the Sala degli Specchi, was part of the formal reception rooms that were originally divided into ten areas, decorated between 1811 and 1814 with elaborate stuccoes, marbles, and ornaments; these were totally altered during the period of the kings of the house of Savoy, who had the vaults repainted in a style more in keeping with the time. The present project is the work of Ignazio Perricci; the ceiling is decorated with an allegory of dance.

Palazzo Pallavicini Rospigliosi

The largest thermal baths in Rome, created on the orders of the emperor Constantine, stood on the site that is today occupied by the Palazzo Pallavicini on the Quirinal Hill near the temple of Serapis. The surviving ruins of those grandiose imperial baths inspired such artists and theoreticians as Sebastiano Serlio and Andrea Palladio until the area fell into the possession of Scipione Borghese. He thought it expedient to have them razed to make room for a home where he could spend the summer months near his uncle, Paul V. Known as Monte Cavallo because of the two sculptural groups of the Dioscuri with their horses, then believed to be the work of Phidias and Praxiteles, that were located at the center of the Piazza Quirinal, this area had been popular with nostalgic humanists since the late Middle Ages.

Work on the building began in 1611 under the direction of Flaminio Ponzio, busy at the same time with work on the Villa Borghese on the Pincian Hill. Jan (Giovanni) van Santen (Giovanni Vasanzio) was asked to design the large garden, which then extended up to the basilica of

The collection in the Palazzo Pallavicini Rospigliosi is one of the best surviving examples of artistic patronage in Rome. The collection was assembled by the Pallavicini family, originally from Liguria, and by the Rospigliosi, the family of Clement IX. Following the joining of the two families, the collection was placed under legal protection. Early in the twentieth century the Rospigliosi portion was sold to the Federation dei Consorzi Agrari.

Santa Maria Maggiore. At the death of Ponzio, in 1613, direction of the work was entrusted to Carlo Maderno, who finished the building following the Renaissance module of a central rectangular body flanked by two wings. Between 1611 and 1612, many of the painters most in vogue had made frescoes in the palace for Scipione. Guido Reni and Paul Bril decorated the loggia on the ground floor with putti. In a style much in keeping with the realistic architecture of paintings by Viviano Codazzi, this country residence was surrounded by

PAGES 164–165: The portrait room includes images of the many people who have owned the palace, from Scipione Borghese to the Altemps family, the Bentivoglio family, Cardinal Mazarin, and finally the Pallavicini Rospigliosi, today's owners.

orchards and vineyards and blended city elements with loggias and porticoes. Each of the three levels of the park had a casino, or lodge, the last of which, destroyed when Via Nazionale was opened, had frescoes by Ludovico Cigoli that are today preserved in Palazzo Braschi.

Reversals in the family fortune forced the Borghese to sell the villa to the Altemps family in 1612, who sold it in turn to the Bentivoglio family in 1619. In exile from Bologna with the Este court of Ferrara, Cardinal Guido Bentivoglio had found himself transferred to Rome to perform various prestigious services for the pontifical court. These services eventually came to include acting as director of the Inquisition and signing the condemnation of Galileo. Learned men, great lovers of beauty, Cardinal Guido and his brother Enzo Bentivoglio nourished a particular love for the arts. Ambitious collectors, they had an enormous effect on the direction taken by popular taste because of the influence they exercised on the artistic decisions made by the rich, generous, but all too often less than learned men who were the first popes of the seventeenth century. They were both attracted to the "modern" style and met its leading proponents. Giudo, distinguished for his simple life and spiritual asceticism, had his portrait painted in 1623 by Van Dyck. Enzo assembled an outstanding painting collection in the

A number of rooms were refurbished and splendidly decorated in the eighteenth century.

palace and became the first admirer of the young French landscapist Claude Lorrain. Taken under the powerful wings of the Bentivoglio brothers, Lorrain rapidly rose to fame, entering the circle of Urban VIII, for whom he painted two radiant imaginary views. Known for his expert judgment, Enzo advised Paul V in his greedy quest for masterpieces and offered guidance to Taddeo Barberini and Gregory XV. The painter Andrea Camassei, an Umbrian follower of Domenichino, lived in the palace, decorating a room with scenes inspired by Love and Psyche.

A letter from the cardinal to the Florentine painter Giovanni da San Giovanni offers a perfect illustration of the cardinal's straightforward approach as an art buyer: "Giovanni, I want you to paint some seascapes with sea battles between monsters and sirens above these unfinished vaults." Between 1622 and 1627, the Florentine artist painted the fanciful *Chariot of the Night*, assisted by Francesco Furini, in one room and frescoed three others on the ground floor with classical rapes— Europa, Amphitrite, and Prosperpine—along with a ceiling fresco of *Perseus Holding the Head of Medusa*; on the *piano nobile* he painted another ceiling fresco, *The Death of Cleopatra*. In the loggias of the ground floor Filippo Napoletano made landscape frescoes and Bonzi Pietro Paolo made some of the still

lifes for which he is also known as Gobbo dei Frutti.

A few years before the death of Cardinal Guido, the Bentivoglio family was forced to sell the villa, the buyers this time being the Lante family; in 1644 the Lantes sold it in turn to the powerful French cardinal Jules

Mazarin. The cardinal had the rooms sumptuously decorated, part of his adroit campaign of artistic patronage, clearly aimed at finding the

Mordecai Weeping before the Palace Gate of Ahasuerus (La Derelitta), once considered a work by Botticelli, was acquired by Prince Giuseppe Rospigliosi in 1816 as a painting of Rhea Silvia by Masaccio; according to Federico Zeri, author of a major catalog of the collection, and other art historians, it is instead an early work by Filippino Lippi.

best artists in Rome and then packing them off to France. He put the palace at the disposal of French guests in Rome and was obviously quite proud of his possession. A little later he commissioned Martino Longhi II to enlarge the princely dwelling and give it a triumphant facade that would be suitably grand and audacious in order to make his social ascent and power perfectly clear to the Roman prelates who had humiliated him in the past. Amid the vicissitudes of fate, and surrounded on all sides by enemies, the famous cardinal succeeded in assembling an extraordinary collection, known to us from an inventory he had drawn up. This reveals the marked interest he showed for secular and erotic scenes, a passion that led his detractors to accuse him of favoring *"les images lascives."*

In 1704 the palace was acquired by the Mancini, Mazarin's last heirs, and was divided between the Rospigliosi and Pallavicini families. The Pallavicini still occupy the palace, maintaining its exceptional painting collection. Their property includes the topmost of the garden's three outbuildings, or casinos, the one known as the Casino dell'Aurora, with frescoes by Guido Reni, as well as other, smaller buildings scattered across the rolling grounds, including, alongside a large semicircular fountain on the central terrace, the so-called loggia of the Muses, decorated with the beautiful *Nine Muses*, the figures painted by

Orazio Gentileschi in an illusionistic setting by Agostino Tassi. The loggia on the ground floor of the palace, today the headquarters of the Federazione Italiana dei Consorzi Agrari, was painted by Paul Bril, famous for his stage-set landscapes and his animals, with a pergola hung with grapes and crowded with birds and butterflies. Guido Reni framed enormous vases of flowers with putti. Closed in by its high walls, Palazzo Pallavicini Rospigliosi has a distinct atmosphere. Since the dawn of the baroque it has been inhabited by collectors and

The collection of art works begun by Lazzaro Pallavicini numbers more than five hundred pieces of truly outstanding importance. The nucleus of Emilian and Bolognese works was collected while he was serving as papal legate in Bologna, but additions were made to the collection following family marriages to members of the Colonna and Lante della Rovere families.

patrons of great art, and visitors to the palace today cannot help but sense some of that extraordinary creative energy. The art collection itself, begun by Cardinal Lazzaro Pallavicini and enriched through marriages with the Colonna family, the Lante della Rovere, and the Rospigliosi, is today on view in the palace on Monte Cavallo. Its five hundred works of enormous importance include paintings by Botticelli, Guercino, Van Dyck, Velázquez, Lorrain, and Reni.

ABOVE AND LEFT: The palace contains many important marble and bronze sculptures, including works by Pierre Puget and Giuseppe Mazzuoli. Paul Bril and Guido Reni decorated the loggia with putti and landscapes in 1612, and Giovanni da San Giovanni made several elaborate ceiling decorations, but few of the palace's original decorations survive.

OPPOSITE: The rooms of the *piano nobile* present vivid testimony to the taste of a large family that is celebrated in the annals of baroque Rome. The quality and opulence of the tapestries, eighteenth-century Roman furniture, porcelain vases, silver, and various decorative objects reflect the status of one of the great papal families and evoke the original atmosphere of the baroque collection.

Casino dell'Aurora

A large park studded with small buildings surrounded the palace that Cardinal Scipione Borghese had built for himself in the seventeenth century on the Quirinal Hill. One of those small buildings is the Casino dell'Aurora. It is set on the Italian-style terraces that mark off the gradations of the slope, skillfully softening any sense of its inclination. The wide arcades of the building open on to the branches of the surrounding trees. Very little has survived of the complex scenery that the cardinal's favorite architect, Giovanni Vasanzio (Jan, or Giovanni, van Santen), planned for his patron's earthly delights, but the loggia designed to provide the cardinal with moments of restful contemplation still stands unchanged. The building's facade is set with antique marbles, and the building itself is just a single large hall flanked by two smaller rooms. Scipione used the Villa Borghese on the Pincian to display his art collection, and it was, in a sense, no more than a kind of private museum; the palace on the Quirinal was altogether different, for he actually lived in it.

The decoration of the

A nymphaeum surrounded by a double staircase decorated with statues stands in front of the Casino dell'Aurora, which was built by Giovanni Vasanzio for the pleasure-loving Scipione Borghese on the highest terrace of the rambling Italian-style garden. The airy pavilion is composed of only three rooms on a single floor, but its exterior is enlivened by abundant decoration composed of ancient relics set harmoniously into the walls.

Farnese gallery by the Carracci led to the large-scale migration to Rome of other artists of the Bologna school. Attracted by the new style employed by these artists, Cardinal Scipione Borghese commissioned Guido Reni (1575–1642) and Domenichino (1581–1641) in 1608 to make frescoes in the oratory of Sant'Andrea in San Gregorio Magno. Satisfied with this work, he then entrusted Guido and several other Bolognese artists, including Giovanni Lanfranco, Francesco Albani, and Antonio Carracci, to redecorate the chapel of the Annunciation in the Quirinal. Guido Reni began work on the vault

of the Casino dell'Aurora in 1613; his *Apollo on the Chariot of the Sun Surrounded by the Hours and Aurora* proved to be his most prestigious commission, the masterpiece of his period in Rome. On the central vault, in an "extreme, rarefied, and suspended" fresco, he expressed in painting the new ideals of classicism. Until the last years of the nineteenth century, learned travelers on their pilgrimage through Italy knelt before this work, which was thought to rank on the same level as the Sistine Chapel and Raphael's Vatican Stanze. Jacob Burckhardt called it the "perfection of two centuries of painting." To please

The large Serlian lodge, which originally looked onto a garden, is flanked by two projecting wings, which house the two smaller side rooms decorated by Giovanni Baglione and Domenico Cresti (known as Passignano), with stories of Rinaldo and Armida.

his hedonistic client Reni sought to capture the true essence of beauty. Aurora (Dawn) is suspended in a clear sky; behind her are the Sun and Apollo's chariot, drawn by its chargers. Apollo sits surrounded by the beautiful Muses, an emblem himself of distilled beauty, praised exuberantly over the centuries. No attempts were made to connect the painting to its surrounding environment— no illusionistic perspective, no minor scenes—and the fresco has the sense of being a separate entity, isolated against the pale background of the vault and marked off by a stucco frame. It is very much a painting taken from a gallery and applied to a wall.

Alongside Reni, Antonio Tempesta painted friezes with *The Triumph of Death and Famine*, and Paul Bril, a precursor of classical Roman landscape painting destined for great fortune during the seventeenth century, presented the story of the Four Seasons by way of the metamorphosis of nature. The paintings in the two side rooms presented themes taken from the story of Rinaldo and Armida, popular characters from Tasso's *Jerusalem Delivered*. In 1614 Giovanni Baglione painted *Rinaldo and Armida*, and Domenico Cresti, known as Domenico Passignano, a Florentine painter very active during the pontificate of Paul V, painted the *Battle of Rinaldo and Armida*.

Standing before the *Aurora*, Charles de Brosses (1709–1777), the learned French magistrate and writer who left us his *Lettres d'Italie*, felt that nothing else he had ever seen was better conceived or more gracious. It was, he said, enchanting.

Following the vicissitudes of the Borghese family, the Casino became the property of the Bentivoglio family before passing to Cardinal Mazarin and then becoming part of the belongings of the Ligurian Pallavicini family in 1704, who still own it.

Guido Reni's fresco of the *Chariot of Apollo Preceded by Aurora* was greeted with such enthusiasm by contemporaries that its name was applied to the casino of Scipione Borghese. Made by Reni between 1613 and 1614, the work seems to bring to life the model of ideal of beauty as incarnated by Raphael and Correggio.

Palazzo Chigi Odescalchi

The magnificent palace that was built opposite the Church of the Santi Apostoli has seen many changes over time, changes in its appearance, but also changes in its name in accordance with the succession of families that, whether because of fate or papal munificence, lived in it and sought to affirm their social status by the splendid architectural work they lavished on it. The original building was the property of the Colonna princes, unrivaled rulers of this quarter of the city. Little remains today of that structure, which was probably turreted, for its appearance changed over time in keeping with the rank and riches of its successive owners.

The building experienced its first complete overhaul at the hands of Carlo Maderno after the year 1622, when ownership of the building passed from the Colonna family to the Ludovisi, as recorded by Baglione in his *Vite* ("Lives"). The short time (1622–28) that Cardinal Ludovico Ludovisi lived in the palace was nonetheless long enough for him to leave his mark on the structure. He turned to his favorite architect, Maderno, who had

RIGHT: The corbels support the monumental windows on the ground floor.

BELOW: The papal coat of arms of the Odescalchi family stands over the divided pediment of a window above the main entrance in the Bernini facade. The facade of the former Chigi Palace was enlarged by Nicola Salvi and Luigi Vanvitelli, creating a double entry.

OPPOSITE: The elaborate decoration in the series of rooms on the *piano nobile* was executed by minor artists, but is highly representative of the refined taste of the baroque period.

already built him a superb villa on the Pincian Hill. During the few years of the cardinal's stay, Maderno designed the large courtyard, which has stood unchanged through all subsequent transformations. In his chronicle of the period, Lione Pascoli recalls how he "beautifully restored the building, having also redone its courtyard," surrounding the broad area with a splendid portico supported by columns and pilasters of the Doric order. The arcades were decorated by numerous statues, including two, representing the late emperors Julian and Maximianus, that have survived to today. In 1628, Cardinal Ludovisi was nominated vice-chancellor and decided to move into a new home, so he sold the palace back to the Colonna princes, who, in 1657, gave it away again, this time to members of the up-and-coming Chigi family from Siena, descendants of "The Magnificent" banker

The ceilings are carved and decorated with gilt rosettes, a style that was much in vogue in Rome during the sixteenth century.

Agostini, owner of the Villa Farnesina.

A learned man, highly respected by all, Fabio Chigi was elected pope as Alexander VII (1655–67) without the usual support of nephew-cardinals. Despite his good intentions, however, he soon found himself forced to give in to the usual nepotistic practices, handing out favors to members of his family. Speaking in this regard, the Jesuit father Onori declared that not summoning one's relatives would have been a sin. Alexander gave in and conformed to Roman customs. His brother Mario became an administrator in the food office while his nephew Flavio was named cardinal and received through the will of Pompeo Colonna the use of the palace opposite Santi Apostoli. Another nephew, Agostino, lived in the building while awaiting his marriage in 1658 to Maria Virginia Borghese.

Despite the financial difficulties the Papal State was then experiencing,

Alexander VII was able to re-model the face of Rome, promoting an astonishing burst of construction that was in large part responsible for the predominantly baroque appearance the city still has. Noted art historian Richard Krautheimer wrote, "None of the other builder popes, from Julius II to Sixtus V to Urban VIII, changed the face and image of Rome as did Alexander VII." The star of this construction program was Bernini, once again occupying a triumphant place on the Roman scene and addressing important projects, such as the ambitious colonnades of St. Peter's.

Interested in having the facade of the palace reworked, the pope's nephew Mario contacted the great architect. Bernini's facade has been altered by later reworkings, but its original appearance is documented by eighteenth-century prints and by the prominent central body of the building. Numerous proposals were presented to the owner before he finally opted for Bernini's design. In fact, he had an unusual wealth of alternatives at his disposal, as indicated by documents preserved in the Chigi Archives of the Biblioteca Apostolica Vaticana. In 1664 he chose Bernini's proposal, the sketches for which were prepared by Bernini's brother Luigi and Carlo Fontana, effective designer of the work since he was at that time head architect of the Bernini workshop. A document of February 7, 1664, attests to

The carved wood decorations above the doors are a highly illustrative example of this rococo type of decoration.

the presence on the site of the great Bernini himself, but his presence in the city of Rome was soon interrupted by his journey to France to present his plans for the Louvre. A letter from Flavio Chigi informs the architect of the satisfying progress of the work: "The facade of my house, with the efforts taken by your brother Luigi, comes along felicitously." The building was given a tripartite face with the central part projecting in accordance with Bernini's design, thus establishing a model that would have great influence on the architecture of central Europe, particularly Vienna. Divided by pilasters of a colossal order, the facade, with its monumental and classical lines, paid homage to both Palladio and Michelangelo. A balustrade, decorated with sculptures today lost, crowned the building above. The overall impression was one of sober elegance, worthy of the home of the descendants of the wonderful Renaissance prince Agostino, as can be seen in a view of the building, made at the conclusion of the work by Giovanni Battista Falda, the printmaker whose works celebrated Pope Alexander VII's efforts in the renovation of Rome.

In keeping with sixteenth-century tradition, Flavio Chigi was a passionate collector of marble relics. Following his death, the precious collection he had assembled was sold in Dresden.

Bernini's efforts in the field of civil architecture met

The four lunettes decorated with marine scenes by Agostino Tassi follow a perspective style much in vogue during the seventeenth century and probably date to the period during which Tassi stayed in the palace of Cardinal Ludovisi.

unlucky or just unhappy fates. Most of the projects he designed were grossly reworked, as was the case with both the Chigi and Montecitorio palaces; others were forever laid aside, the prime example of this fate being his unfortunate plans for the Louvre. Just as he had hoped to design an ideal suburban home for the Barberini family, he had hoped to create for the Chigi family a true city palace, a noble palace in the style of the late baroque.

In 1746, when the Chigis moved into a new home in Piazza Colonna, the palace opposite the Church of the Santi Apostoli was bought by Prince Baldassare Odescalchi, great-grandson of Innocent XI (1676–91). In 1750 he commissioned Nicolò Salvi and Luigi Vanvitelli to enlarge the palace and give it some new luster. To better compete with the Colonna family, whose property stood on the opposite side of the piazza, the two architects elongated the facade, undoing Bernini's design. They added two doors in the wings at the sides, each door crowned by a balcony and a coat of arms—four bands of silver accompanied by a lion, six incense holders, and a crowned eagle.

Most of the sumptuous furnishings designed for the palace have been lost. Also gone are the paintings and sculpture, and the tapestries made after designs by Giulio Romano and Peter Paul Rubens that decorated the apartments of Prince Livio

The palace is decorated with a rich collection of statues collected by Flavio Chigi, a great connoisseur of objects of antiquity. Many pieces of furniture have been removed from the palace, including a famous bed designed by Johann Paul Schor.

early in the eighteenth century, apartments later inhabited by Queen Mary Casimir, widow of John III of Poland, during her visit to Rome. Gone, too, is Cardinal Chigi's spectacular bed, designed by the German painter Johann Paul Schor and covered in white satin painted with floral motifs. The Genoese painter Giovanni Battista Gaulli (1639–1709) also worked here, narrating on the walls of an alcove a *Fable of Endymion* now in the Chigi Palace in Piazza Colonna. There is also the painting by Caravaggio showing the *Conversion of Paul*, which came to Rome by way of the inheritance of the Genoese collection of Balbi of Piovera.

A fire that destroyed much of the upper floor of the building in 1887 led to the palace's most recent transformation. Raffaele Ojetti was commissioned to design a new facade for the Odescalchi property on Via del Corso, and he created the rusticated facade we see today. Its design, very much in keeping with the eclectic trends of those years, is based on a neo-Renaissance Florentine style.

ABOVE: The Hall of Cybele.

OPPOSITE: The vault with the fresco of Cybele seated on a carriage drawn by two lions may be attributable to the painter Girolamo Curti, known as Dentone. The fresco was mentioned by Malvasia, and was made at the time of Cardinal Ludovisi.

Palazzo Altieri

The Altieri family traced their lineage back to the days of Aeneas and owned buildings in Rome's Pigna quarter as early as the fourteenth century, but it was only in the seventeenth century, after one of their members, Emilio Altieri, was elected pope as Clement X (1670–76) that the family replaced its simple homes with a suitably substantial palace. This stood on land directly opposite the Church of the Gesù, the Jesuits' principal church in Rome. The Altieri had been slowly buying up buildings around the square, which in fact originally bore their name, as can be seen on the map by Bufalini dating to 1551. The square later came to be called Piazza del Gesù, however, for the Jesuits were steadily extending their dominion into Altieri territory, such that they inevitably came into conflict with that well-to-do family, which claimed to have been living there, in the very heart of republican Rome, since time immemorial. This hostility grew only stronger when the Jesuits saw the grandiose palace being constructed so near their church. While the family's claim to descend from a certain

RIGHT AND BELOW: In 1650, the architect De' Rossi began rebuilding and enlarging the home of the ancient Altieri family.

OPPOSITE: The grand staircase eventually became the unifying element between the old and new buildings, providing the connection between the two enormous courtyards.

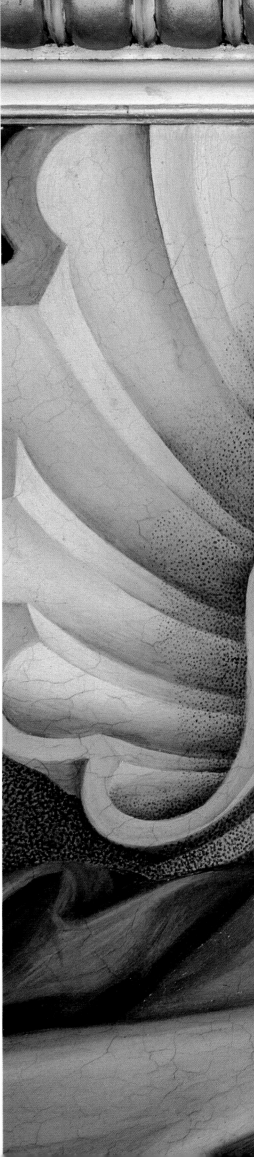

ancient Lucius Alterius hardly seemed credible, it is certainly true that in 1330 Giacomo Alterius, "aside from jousting with bulls in the Colosseum," had bought a first house near Santa Maria degli Astalli.

The original nucleus of today's palace was built at the request of Cardinal Giovanni Battista Altieri during the Holy Year celebrations in

1650. The cardinal had initially turned to Carlo Fontana, a student of Bernini much in vogue at the time among the powerful, and Fontana drew up plans, but these plans were put aside, and the commission went instead to Giovanni Angonio de' Rossi (1616–1695), an architect who later enjoyed great professional success, becoming

ABOVE: The fresco made by Fabrizio Chiari in 1675, in the central octagon of the vault of the Sala degli Specchi, presents the Chariot of the Sun.

OPPOSITE: In 1675, Fabrizio Chiari created a band of painted decorations, including this detail, around the upper wall of the Sala degli Specchi.

involved in a variety of large-scale endeavors and rising to be one of the leading architects in Rome during the late seventeenth century.

The original building was probably finished by the time of the cardinal's death in 1654. Then came the election of Clement X and the family's decision to enlarge the palace and incorporate into it various holdings that they had acquired around the square. One of Emilio's brothers was unexpectedly made a cardinal himself, on April 28, 1670, when almost on the point of death, and he bequeathed 18,000 scudi toward the restoration of the palace. For this new work the family again turned to Giovanni Antonio de' Rossi.

When he returned to the site in 1670, Giovanni Antonio de' Rossi was well established and well to do. He planned the enlargement of the building following a plan designed to incorporate the entire city block, creating a single grandiose structure. The building was also to be embellished and brought up to date stylistically. The portal, surmounted by the family's coat of arms, opened onto an elegant courtyard with a cornice covered by heraldic stars and turtles. In these plans the architect created his own language, a combination of the classical and the baroque. The main stairway is sober and elegant, following harmonious proportions and illuminated by large windows. The stairway's niches were decorated with

LEFT AND BELOW: The Noble Cabinet is divided from the Sala degli Specchi by a doorway with mirrors in alabaster flanked by a pair of columns in porphyry.

OPPOSITE: The ceiling fresco, made in 1673 by Carlo Maratti, showing the *Allegory of Clemency*, was the most prestigious and important commission in Rome in the second half of the century. It marked a change in taste across Europe, and its affirmation of the classical became the model for later decorations in royal palaces all across Europe. The standing figure of Public Felicity has the features of Gasparo Altieri, the pope's adopted nephew, who was authorized to continue the family name.

antique sculptures from the collection begun by Marc Antonio Altieri. This part of the construction thus came into being twenty years after the building made for the cardinal and was merged with it, the two monumental courtyards being joined.

These plans had been made possible by the ascent to the throne of St. Peter of Clement X, but a great deal of urgency was involved since the pope was then eighty years old. The Altieri family rushed to get the building completed, enlarging it beyond all proportion and carrying on so much they aroused the sarcasm of Pasquino, who compared their building fury to that which had possessed the emperor Nero at time of his Golden House. Fearing that the pope did not have long to live, the family members grew desperate to complete the ambitious palace at all costs, ordering that work should continue through the night, the construction site being illuminated by blazing torches. All this gave rise to scandal, and the pope felt it necessary to disassociate himself from the project. The old palace was used to keep up appearances, while the new extensions were fitted out as the home of Pope Clement X's nephew Cardinal Paluzzo Paluzzi degli Albertoni. In this way a complex and spacious new building came into being, planned in large part under the direct and attentive gaze of its owner, who oversaw the con-

version of the home "from cardinal's palace to the seat of the court of a papal family." As the last male member of the Altieri family, the pope had adopted the Roman nobleman Gasparo Paluzzo degli Albertoni, and it was Gasparo's uncle, Paluzzo Paluzzi degli Albertoni, who

directed the construction of this new building. It was thus not without a certain irony that the ancient family line of the Altieri experienced the moment of its greatest glory at the precise moment of its extinction, which can be said to have begun with the adop-

BELOW: The ceiling of the Summer Bedroom was decorated by Felice Giani. The central scene is of Paris and Helen.

OPPOSITE: The vault of the Winter Bedroom, also known as the Sala dei Trionfi, was frescoed with triumphal processions by Giuseppe Cades.

PAGE 202: The marble frieze that runs along the room shows games among putti, and was made by Vincenzo Pacetti in 1788.

PAGE 203: The Noble Cabinet, also called the Sala del Mosaico, was richly decorated in the 1790s. Built by the architect Giuseppe Barberi, it represents one of the most beautiful neoclassical interiors in Rome. Above the alabaster doors is Tarpeia offering the keys of the Campidoglio to Taxio, painted by Antonio Cavallucci in 1791.

tion of Paluzzo. The cardinal's apartment was in the new wing, of course, its walls covered by stuccoes by Ercole Ferrata and precious fabrics. The halls were done up with enormous splendor. The roomy, sunny areas were in sharp contrast to the old-fashioned, somber rooms of Cardinal Giovanni Battista Altieri, who had expressed the desire for decoration "darkly shaded, suitable for the memory of ancestors," rather than anything that would glorify the power of the new Altieri.

The monumental decorative cycle began halfway into the seventeenth century and was carried on for a century, even a little longer, progressively covering the numerous rooms. The main theme was the celebration of Rome, ancient and modern, Christian and pagan. Don Carlo Altieri sought advice from Cardinal Camillo Massimo and Giovanni Bellori, initially entrusting the decoration to the leading artist in Rome at that time, Carlo Maratti. The great hall was ready to be frescoed in 1673, and its ceiling offered ample space for the painter's skilled allegories. The chosen theme, the *Allegory of Clemency*, an allusion to the pope's name, was designed to glorify that person. This room's decoration came to represent the most prestigious and influential commission of the second half of the century in Rome, and it proved the perfect dividing line for a change in taste, with the triumph of the classical—what the artist himself had wanted—thus becoming a model for the later decoration of royal palaces throughout Europe. The standing figure of Public

Felicity has the features of Gasparo Altieri, the pope's adopted nephew. He had been made heir on condition that the children of his marriage to Altieri's niece and sole heir, Laura Caterina, would bear the Altieri name. At the same time, in 1675, work was begun on the sumptuous baroque decoration of the Sala Rossa, its lunettes and vault painted by Nicolò Berrettoni, the Sala degli Specchi, decorated by Fabrizio Chiari, and the Sala Verde, with frescoes by Francesco Cozza presenting *Allegories of Autumn and Winter.* The entire *piano nobile* was reworked. Distinctive furniture was specially designed for the space, most of it now dispersed. The Bolognese artist Domenico Canuti filled the walls of the room overlooking Piazza del Gesù with a vast fresco presenting the *Origins of Rome.* The painting collection, with its marked classical sensibility, assembled in strict accordance with the dictates of Giovanni Bellori, included paintings by Correggio and Veronese, Perugino and Guido Reni. Prized marbles covered the walls in a profusion of Sicilian jasper and black-and-white and cipolin marble. Crystal, gold, silver, and mirrors were assembled to create a theatrical setting. The splendor of the decoration extended even to the floors, which were covered with mosaics of brick and then mosaics of stonework. The walls not frescoed were hung with costly damasks, decorated

velvets, and brocades. An extraordinary library held 13,000 precious volumes arranged on shelves of carved walnut, following a design by De' Rossi himself.

At the turn of the new century, following the deaths of Paluzzo and Clement X, Gasparo Altieri decided to leave Rome for Venice, thus bringing an end to all acquisitions. In 1735, his son, Girolamo, began the work again with the renovation of several of the halls facing onto the main courtyard in the palace built back in the 1650s for Cardinal Giovanni Battista Altieri. This was when the baroque drawing room came into being. The last great series of decorations in the palace was made under the direction of Girolamo's son, Emilio Carlo, himself a painter and connoisseur of art as well as the sponsor of archaeological excavations along the Tiber River. The occasion was the celebration of the wedding of the first-born Paluzzo with Marianne of Saxony. Felice Giani was summoned to create, as a kind of swan song, a narration of "vaporous and fleeting" fables. In so doing, he demonstrated a perfect understanding of the wishes of his client. The architect Giuseppe Barberi created the Noble Cabinet, which represents one of the most beautiful neoclassical settings in Rome. Rome, of course, was the cradle of the neoclassical style, which came into being, it has been said, as a result of "the brilliant conspiracy of

Niccolò Berrettoni decorated the vault in the Sala Rossa with frescoes in 1675; at the center is the *Allegory of Love.*

enthusiastic geniuses joined there from every corner of Europe." The leading artists of the city, brought together by their passion for the ancient, were joined in the eighteenth-century rooms in Palazzo Altieri. The theme of the birth of Romulus, son of the god Mars and Rhea Silvia, is an allusion to the spouses, and a mosaic floor from the Augustan age, uncovered in Ostia in 1783, was placed in the center of the floor. The various artists succeeded in giving a harmonious sense to the decoration of stuccoes, marbles, and frescoes around the central painting by Stefano Tofanelli showing the *Glorification of Romulus*. Vincenzo Pacetti carved the frieze of dancing putti while Felice Giani painted the grotesques on the walls together with Peter, author of the animals; Basconi, the flowers; and Giovanni Campovecchio, the landscapes. The panels over the doors, by Antonio Cavallucci, Giuseppe Cades, Francesco Manno, and Anton von Maron, narrate the legend of the rape of the Sabine women. One then enters the Winter Bedroom, frescoed in 1789 by the great master of decoration Felice Giani with floral motifs and grotesques and with the series of triumphs of Eros, Prosperity, Venus, and the Arts. The Oval Boudoir was frescoed by the master and his students with the story of Atalanta and Hippomenes, Diana and Actaeon, and the judgment of Paris. The

final room, the Summer Bedroom, brought this sophisticated decorative cycle, full of lightness and verve, to a close. Giani created a new decor of rarefied Hellenistic grace in which, inspired by the magical beauty of the walls, it would have been easy to entertain a lover, in

keeping with the spirit of sensual liberties of the Age of Enlightenment. Fleeing the pompous grandeur of the seventeenth-century apartments of Cardinal Paluzzo, Giani offered his client intimacy and escape in the arcane world of mythology as captured and presented in the style of Pompeiian painting. He created smaller spaces, splendid alcoves to suit princes increasingly sensitive to the decoration of every corner of every room.

ABOVE: A recently decorated overdoor pediment.

OPPOSITE: The famous soffit of the Oval Boudoir, painted with a *Triumph of Love* by Felice Giani and his students.

Palazzo Doria Pamphili

The Doria Pamphili Palace physically incorporates several ancient buildings, and its history, in a similar fashion, weaves together events from the stories of several noble families. The palace's importance today seems tied more than ever to the magnificent art collection that has been displayed in its enormous gallery since the eighteenth century. Closely tied by two marriages to the Aldobrandini and Doria families, the Pamphili family slowly put together the complex we see today, which can be entered by way of six monumental entrances leading to five courtyards.

Prince Camillo Pamphili (1622–1666), nephew of Innocent X, acquired the first holding after returning from a short stay in Avignon as papal legate. A papal brief of Alexander VII, dated May 26, 1659, had directed the Jesuit fathers of the Collegio Romano to enlarge the piazza by buying the Salviati palace and demolishing part of it. Complying with the precocious urban-planning intention, Camillo began building within a year. To direct the work he called on Antonio del Grande, a follower of

OPPOSITE: The courtyard of the palace dates to the early sixteenth-century period of the building, which was constructed by a Sorrentino cardinal around 1440 and then restored and enlarged by Giovanni Fazio Santoro in the early years of the sixteenth century. It became the property of Cardinal Pietro Aldobrandini in 1606 and then passed on to the Pamphili princes following the marriage of Olimpia Aldobrandini to Camillo Pamphili. The fourth side of the colonnade was added only during the operations directed by Gabriele Valvassori in the 1730s, at which time the second floor of the colonnade was closed off with windows in the rococo style.

Girolamo Rainaldi, and architect of the gallery in Palazzo Colonna. Thus began the complex adventure of the Island of the Pamphili, the result of the agglomeration of at least five phases of construction.

A patron of Borromini and Alessandro Algardi, Camillo hoped to construct a suitable building in which to house the works of art that he was so avidly collecting. His uncle Innocent X (1644–55) demonstrated little interest in art, but he did commission Veláz- quez to paint his portrait,

LEFT: The palace's chapel was de- signed between 1689 and 1691 by Carlo Fontana for Cardinal Bene- detto Pamphili; it was restored by Francesco Nicoletti during the second half of the eighteenth century and further reworked in the middle of the nineteenth century by Andrea Busiri Vici.

BELOW: The wing of the palace that runs along Via del Corso, known as the Galleria degli Specchi, was decorated after the open loggia overlooking the sixteenth-century courtyard was closed by Gabriele Valvassori in 1734.

LEFT: The bust of Innocent X by Gian Lorenzo Bernini stands in one corner of the gallery beside the famous portrait of the pope made by Velázquez.

OPPOSITE: The Labors of Hercules are a recurrent theme in the palace's decorations. They were presented on the vault of the Galleria degli Specchi by Aureliano Milani, who painted the scene of Hercules shooting the centaur Nessus. Between 1767 and 1769, the team of artists that decorated most of the gallery was headed by the two "ornamentalist painters" Pietro Bernabò and Giovanni Angeloni.

today judged perhaps the most beautiful portrait of the seventeenth century and displayed in the gallery. For his part, Camillo Pamphili brought about a notable artistic reawakening in the city for, although capricious, as the biographer Giovanni Battista Passeri recalls, "He gave painters and sculptors more opportunities for work, as well as for torment, than any other person in his time." He was indeed headstrong. He got his uncle to nomi-

nate him cardinal, but then changed his mind and decided to marry, which meant, of course, that he had to renounce the purple robes, which required following a quite complex procedure. It was a truly princely marriage, however. In 1647 he wed Olimpia Aldobrandini, princess of Rossano (1623–1681), thus laying the groundwork for an opulent dynasty since Olimpia brought immense wealth as her dowry. As the widow of Paolo Borghese she

also brought her husband, aside from an important art collection, the palace next door to the church of Santa Maria in Via Lata. This had been built by a Sorrentino cardinal around 1440 and then restored and enlarged by Giovanni Fazio Santoro during the first years of the sixteenth century, when it was praised by Julius II. Ownership then passed to the Della Rovere family, who further embellished it before handing it on to Cardinal

Pietro Albobrandini, nephew of Clement VIII, in 1601. To decorate a chapel flanking the church, he asked Annibale Carracci to make the celebrated lunettes on canvas that are today preserved in the gallery. The inventory of the Aldobrandini collection, compiled by Monsignor Giovan Battista Agucchi in 1603, documents the extraordinary nucleus of paintings, including the *Salome* by Titian and the Este collection of Ferrara paintings.

A series of fifteenth-century buildings, property of Camillo's wife, thus came to be incorporated into the palace of the Collegio Romano, creating the great complex that still belongs to the family. Camillo's son Benedetto inaugurated a series of rooms around the courtyard dedicated to painting. The Stanza dei Quadri is followed by the Stanza degli Animali and finally the much-loved Stanza dei Paesi, full of sunny landscapes by Claude Lorrain and Gaspard Dughet. These works reminded "the amiable but substantially uncultured" prince of the Villa Belrespiro that Algardi had built for him.

Antonio del Grande finished work on the building of the Collegio Romano in 1675. In keeping with seventeenth-century tradition, he made few important changes to the large facade, demonstrating far greater creativity in the broad vestibule, covered by an airy vault of austere severity, that led to the *piano nobile* by way of a stairway deco-

rated with antique statues. The Salone del Pussino, decorated with the rocky, pre-Romantic landscapes of Dughet (known as Pussino because he was the brother-in-law of Nicolas Poussin), led to a series of rooms, the Sala Celeste, Sala del Trono, and Sala dei Velluti, slowly advancing to the rooms of the gallery, which were given their current appearance only much later.

Another wave of splendor washed over these rooms about a century later. Rome had managed to more or less skip over the rococo style without even putting its feet down within it, for the city's baroque heritage was refusing to die; but the city now saw the transformation of the austere facade in Via Lata. In 1731, Prince Don Camillo Pamphili asked one of the few representatives of the rococo style in Rome, Gabriele Valvassori, to rebuild the main facade and integrate it by closing off its open loggia. The palace then took a rich allure, more in harmony with the times. The collection of paintings continued to grow, thanks to the inheritance that the Genoese Doria family left to the Pamphili when their name came to an end following the marriage in 1671 of Anna Pamphili-Landi to Prince Andrea IV Doria. The gallery, covered with Pompeiian decorations by Annibale Angelini, kept up to date with archaeological discoveries.

The Doria Pamphili Palace is the complex architectural

Annibale Carracci,
The Flight into Egypt, c. 1605.

result of several buildings and four centuries blended to create a unified, regal structure. This opulent palace, more than any other palace or place in Rome, offers the opportunity not just to admire works of art but to experience something of the spirit that led to the formation of the great Roman collections, the majority of which are no longer intact. The Doria Pamphili collection of paintings and sculpture has survived across centuries of history and is open to the public thanks to the farsighted efforts of the heirs.

LEFT: In the Salone Aldobrandini are the four tapestries woven in Brussels in the sixteenth century, showing scenes of the battle of Lepanto, in which Giovanni Andrea Doria distinguished himself. There are also numerous archaeological relics from the Pamphili villa on the Janiculum Hill.

OPPOSITE: Many paintings in the Doria Pamphili collection, including this portrait of Innocent X by Velázquez, are arranged along the gallery walls; the order of the paintings was recently changed to match the arrangement in the late eighteenth century, as documented in the archives.

Palazzo Rondinini

The spirit of classical antiquity once pervaded this palace to an almost obsessive degree, testimony to the devotion for things Greco-Roman that gripped wealthy collectors during the eighteenth century and that made Rome once again Europe's most cosmopolitan city. Ever since the Renaissance, architects in Rome were called upon to design buildings for art collectors, and this palace on Via Lata came into being primarily to house such a collection, that of Giuseppe Rondinini, which had, in fact, become an integral part of his very personality. The architect Alessandro Dori kept his client's archaeological obsession very much in mind and used the marquis's taste and erudition in the design of his home, the architecture of which harmoniously blends carved marbles and marble fragments, inscriptions and columns of gray granite, slabs of ancient yellow porphyry and black African porphyry, to the point of inventing its own style of systematic decoration to satisfy this cult of antiquity.

The building dates back to a small palace near the Piazza del Popolo that Margherita

The main staircase, which leads to the *piano nobile*, was designed by the architect Alessandro Dori. It is decorated at the bottom by this ancient sculptural group of a satyr and nymph set in a niche.

Ambra Rondinini, Giuseppe's mother, had bought from the Barnabite fathers of Arpino in 1744.

Giuseppe Cesari, the artist known as Cavaliere d'Arpino (1568–1640), had made this building to serve as his own family residence. His social standing and the artistic fame he had achieved during the pontificate of Clement VIII allowed him, in 1604, to buy for 3,000 scudi an unfinished palace on the Via del Corso. In his *Vite* ("Lives") Baglione mentions the preparatory designs for the palace, which were made by Flaminio Ponzio, Pope Paul V's favorite architect, and the two angels by Andrea Buonvicino that decorated the exterior. The last member of the Cesari family, Giuseppe dei Cesari di Arpino, left the palace to the Barnabite fathers, who sold it shortly afterward to Giuseppe's mother. Nothing remains of this first structure except mentions in chronicles that describe its size.

Originally from Romagna, the Rondinini family had moved to Rome in 1572 to begin a glorious social ascent. While living in Via di Campo Marzio, the original marquis assembled the nucleus of the collection of seventeenth-century paintings. By carefully managing his capital, Giuseppe Rondinini was able to avoid the reversals that impoverished the great majority of Rome's aristocracy. During the second half of the eighteenth century he had the palace restored and organized a magnificent

collection of paintings—unfortunately broken up after his death in 1801—that included some of the best artists of the period but showed a marked fondness for Neapolitan and French painters. Remodeled and enlarged by Alessandro Dori, the palace in Via del Corso was com-

of the monumental, severe, and grandiose. In keeping with the lofty harmonies of the design, the stuccoes repeated images drawn from the collection, and polychrome marbles were used in the intarsia decoration of the floor. A plaque indicates that construction on the palace

PAGE 220: Fragments of classical works appear in all corners of the elaborately decorated courtyard and are inserted in the pilasters leading to the main staircase. In their desire to revive the style of the ancients, eighteenth-century architects made free use of such works from antiquity and mixed them in among their own modern inventions, all in a conscious effort to free the works of antiquity from galleries and museums.

pletely transformed. The body of the building, which extended toward the Church of San Giacomo, was enlarged. In keeping with the new style, according to which the monumental and vast halls of the baroque were to be replaced with smaller, more comfortable rooms, Dori designed highly accessible rooms softened by a new sense of intimacy. As in every patrician palace, one ascended a spacious stairway to a series of large rooms on the *piano nobile*. The detailed but refined decoration of these rooms had nothing in keeping with the old precepts

ended in 1764, and the decoration began.

Goethe, who stayed on the Via del Corso, met "baron Rondinini" and was suitably impressed by his collection. The Swiss painter Angelica Kauffmann mentions seeing several of the works in the diary she kept of her Roman journey. The century was gliding toward new goals. Benedict XIV corresponded with Voltaire and watched over archaeological excavations, blocking the exportation of works of art. Closed in his own world, hostile to change, troubled by the winds of revolution, the marquis

PAGE 221: A door opening onto a series of rooms is carved with elegant rococo motifs and offers a glimpse of a Roman bust.

ABOVE: The vestibule, which has the appearance of a nymphaeum, is surrounded by a cornice supported by telamons (male caryatids) made by the stuccoworker G. Ferrari and by elegant rococo-style elements applied with decorative exuberance.

OPPOSITE: The flight of stairs ends at a door surmounted by a niche bearing this bust of a Roman emperor. The vault is covered by a thick plasterwork decoration of foliage dotted with cupids and swallows—swallows are the heraldic emblem of Giuseppe Rondinini (*rondine* is Italian for "swallow").

Rondinini hid his collection from the eyes of the world and sought shelter in ancient memories.

All but forgotten today, Dori was a highly praised architect in his own time; Pope Clement XIV chose him for the prestigious commission of designing the basis of the Museo Pio-Clementino. His preferred style of architecture was dynamic and theatrical, embellished by a keen pictorial sense. He was capable of harmoniously orchestrating stuccowork and polychrome floor decorations, always opting for the pictorial, in a

style reminiscent of Giovanni Paolo Pannini, the Italian painter known for vast cityscapes blending landmarks of ancient and Renaissance Rome. The collection of antique sculpture was located in a splendid, highly imaginative framework, vigorous and graceful. While demonstrating erudition in the selection of themes solidly related to the passions of his learned client, he was able nonetheless to remain light.

The Capranica family inherited the palace, which then passed to the banker Feoli. The building was rented to the Russian embassy dur-

PAGES 224–225: The marchese Giuseppe Rondinini was so enthralled with antique marbles that the pope grew jealous; many of these works are today displayed in the Gabinetto dei Marmi. The elegant style of decoration that the marchese promoted involved setting the marble relics in niches, which were in turn embellished by antique marbles. The faux wood frames must have alluded to some atelier or antiquarian collection. The floor of inlaid marble in the "Venetian" style appears in most of the rooms on the *piano nobile*, and is itself set with scattered archaeological fragments.

ABOVE: This detail of a bird resting on a balustrade, in the fresco of the vault of the Sala di Anfitrite ed Europa, is the work of an Emilian *quadratura* painter, and represents a style much in vogue at the end of the eighteenth century.

OPPOSITE: The vault of the gallery is decorated with a fresco by Jacques Gamelin, showing the fall of Phaëthon, from 1772.

ing the nineteenth century, and an Orthodox chapel was built that has since disappeared. Since 1946, the owner of the palace has been the Banca Nazionale dell'Agricoltura, which bought it from the last heir of the Sanseverino. The new owners have brought an end to the destruction of the building caused by arbitrary alterations and the scattering of its belongings.

The Rondanini *Pietà* by Michelangelo once stood in the palace's courtyard on a base of travertine marble; today it is in Milan's Castello Sforesco. It is but a single example. A glance at old inventories reveals how the many busts and bas-reliefs once part of the collection were dispersed. But the list of these works alone offers a sense of that old passion, once so total and all-consuming, but no longer tangible now that almost all the statues are long gone, leaving behind not even a trace.

OPPOSITE: The ceiling of the grand ballroom is decorated by a large painting by the Neapolitan artist Corrado Giaquinto, showing Minerva presenting Spain to Jupiter and Juno. Made in 1751, it was brought from the Santa Croce palace in Palermo.

ABOVE: An anteroom decorated with a fountain leads to the great ballroom, which was restored early in the twentieth century, at which time it was decorated with rococo-style monsters made of carved and gilt wood.

Palazzo Orsini Taverna

The ancient fortress of the Orsini family was built on the hill known as Monte Giordano, an area formed by debris swept along and accumulated there during floodings of the Tiber. During its earliest stages this citadel was much like a small, independent town, with its own central piazza surrounded by palaces and its own church, the whole assembly defended by towers with battlements at every corner. This rise overlooking the Tiber had been fortified as a stronghold since early in the Middle Ages for it was an ideal location from which to defend those living nearby from barbarians and marauders. It also became, inevitably, the scene of medieval feuds.

A document dated October 21, 1286, indicates that three brothers of Pope Nicholas III (Giovanni Gaetano Orsini) were living on the hill at that time, each in his own separate home. Before this, the hill had been inhabited by the ancient and noble families of the Boveschi and the Stefaneschi; it was named Monte Giordano after Giordano di Poncello, a courageous follower of the revolutionary Cola di Rienzo (who was killed in 1354).

LEFT: The sturdy outer walls recall the Orsini family's fourteenth-century fortress, as does the Torre Augusta, built late in the nineteenth century by the Taverna counts in memory of the original independent town. Composed of several separate buildings the complex on Monte Giordano had no single overall design for many years of its existence.

OPPOSITE: The broad, elegant main staircase leading to the *piano nobile* was made by Francesco Rust, who was hired by the Gabrielli family to build a wing connecting the palace of the dukes of Bracciano to that of the dukes of Pitigliano.

During the fifteenth century, intrigues, sieges, and battles alternated with periods of pleasant conversation and humanistic studies. In his *Diario*, Stefano Infessura relates that on April 20, 1445, the day of the coronation of Calixtus III (the first Borgia pope), a bloody battle broke out among various members of the Orsini family, which led to a siege by henchmen serving Cesare Borgia. Midway through the sixteenth century Cardinal Ippolito d'Este, life tenant of Prince Camillo, made the palace the site of a splendid court, alternating his stays in Rome with rest periods in the Villa of Tivoli. During this period the palace was regularly visited

by ambassadors and cardinals; the poet Torquato Tasso spent some time there. Chroniclers tell of great celebrations with jugglers and tightrope walkers called in to perform for the benefit of the illustrious guests who stayed in the palace. The courtyard was the setting for mock combats, hunts, and bearbaiting. The exterior of the palace still has the spare and severe Renaissance architectural elements it had under the Orsini. Also dating from that period is the portico, although it has lost "the beautiful stairway decorated with scenes using many figures and with windows closed with alabaster in place of glass," as described by Rucellai in 1450. The power

The neo-Pompeiian decoration of the palace that once belonged to the dukes of Pitigliano was commissioned by Pietro Gabrielli, whose family became the owners of Monte Giordano in 1688. Gabrielli commissioned Liborio Coccetti to prepare new apartments to celebrate the marriage of his son Mario to Charlotte Bonaparte. Coccetti made the decorations between 1809 and 1816, presenting scenes from Etruscan, Roman, and Egyptian mythology.

of the Orsini family, lords of Bracciano, Monterotondo, and Pitigliano, was slowly declining, however, and in 1688 the house on Monte Giordano was sold by court order, and ownership passed to the Gabrielli family.

Prince Pietro Gabrielli did nothing to change the exterior's Renaissance simplicity, turning his attention instead to the interior rooms, which he had transformed into luxurious halls. The three main buildings were partially joined by a new wing, but the essential structure of the complex remained intact. A great connoisseur and passionate collector, the prince had the interior apartments redecorated and frescoed on the occasion of the marriage, in 1815, of his son Mario to Charlotte Bonaparte. The cycle of frescoes was made by the artist Liborio Coccetti (1739–1816), who had requested protection from the prince following certain financial difficulties with the Vatican authorities; in granting him shelter, the prince saved him from the dreaded dungeons of Castel Sant'Angelo. Coccetti worked away passionately to repay his host, but now the palace, despite its luxuries and comforts, became his prison. In everything he did, Coccetti expressed a longing for open vistas and space, painting perspective colonnades that opened skyward and making his escape by way of themes drawn from the Old Testament, primarily Genesis, and from Roman history. Confined to those interiors, he used his time decorating and renewing the *piano nobile*, following the taste of the period. From 1809 to his death in 1816, Coccetti worked alone, a rare instance of individual effort in a period when such decorations were carried out by entire teams of artists, the master conceiving the overall design and working on select areas but leaving the secondary areas and details to the members of his workshop. Coccetti had earlier worked in Umbria and the Latium region and is little known within the artistic panorama of Rome, although he contributed to other palaces in the city, including Palazzo Braschi. The Gabrielli apartments offered him the opportunity to present David dancing beneath the Ark of the Covenant, the prophet Elijah being raised toward heaven in the chariot, Joseph and his brothers, the destruction of Sodom and Gomor-

The walls of the Sala di Camilla, the largest of the apartments decorated by Liborio Coccetti, present gods, rites, and sacrifices.

rah, and the Queen of Sheba. The principal scenes are surrounded with magnificent framing scenes, following a masterful subtlety, the whole spread with a small army of winged putti. Voluptuous angels swoop down from every corner, mixing with faux frames, grisaille work, and trompe l'oeil niches, pilasters, and medallions, while the black-and-carmine backgrounds demonstrate an awareness of Pompeii and Herculaneum interiors. Although locked away in his gilt prison, Coccetti somehow intuited the classical-revival style of the Directoire period, creating works that can be set alongside the mythologies of David and the billowy landscapes of Fragonard.

The Gabrielli family collected precious tapestries and a magnificent series of paintings by Sebastiano Ricci (1659–1734) and Giovanni Battista Pittoni (1687–1767). Vasari speaks of antique-style decorations made by Masolino and Giottino that decorated the walls and that presented portraits of famous men, but these have been lost. According to other sources, some of the halls had been frescoed by Girolamo Muziano and Lodovico Cigoli. Built during the heyday of the *gens Orsina*, the monumental fountain with two pools splashing with water from the Acqua Paola aqueduct was restored in the eighteenth century by Antonio Casoni. Unwise speculations in the building industry

led to the sudden collapse of the Gabrielli fortune, forcing the family to transfer ownership of the palace on Monte Giordano in 1888. The Milanese family of the Taverna counts, relatives of the current owners, acquired the evocative group of buildings. Even today, in part

The Sala di Ocresia, decorated by Coccetti, recounts the legend of the beautiful slave Ocresia. While serving at the court of the Etruscan queen Tanaquil, Ocresia, by placing herself upon a burning hearth, was impregnated by the god Vulcan, thus conceiving the future king Servius Tullius. This tale, related by Ovid in his *Fasti*, gives Rome's sixth king truly noble origins.

because of their undecorated walls and in part because of the remnants of ancient towers, these buildings have something of the severe sense of a fortress.

At the center of the ceiling is a scene depicting the death of the queen of the Volsci being witnessed by Turnus, prince of the Rutulians, an episode drawn from Virgil's *Aeneid*.

The Villas

Guercino, detail of the fresco *Fame, Honor and Virtue* in the Casino Boncompagni Ludovisi.

Villa Chigi, known as La Farnesina

The wealthy Sienese banker Agostino Chigi (c. 1465–1520) selected a spot along the west bank of the Tiber, just outside the walls of the city, as the site for his second residence, a villa in which he planned to lead the life described by the ancients. This villa was to be a place for leisure and cultured conversation, a place for the highest forms of entertainment. Building it would give him a sense of rewarding accomplishment, the same sense of accomplishment that, a century earlier, he would have sought by having a cathedral built.

In 1505, the Sienese painter and architect Baldassare Peruzzi (1481–1536) gave this rural fantasy its exquisitely elegant form. Peruzzi was a scholar of classical antiquity, dedicated most of all to uncovering the secrets of its pleasing and profound harmonies. The exterior of the building, today plastered over, was originally covered with monochrome decorations of fairy-tale gaiety composed of telamons (male caryatids) and plant elements made by Peruzzi himself. Truly neopagan, both in its intentions and its inspiration, the villa draws much

OPPOSITE: The villa's external appearance was much different during the period of Agostino Chigi, when the plaster was covered with graffito decorations of telamons (male caryatids) and plant elements made by Baldassare Peruzzi. The building, which Vasari claimed had been "born, not built," was greatly admired by contemporaries, who saw in it the rebirth of the classical world.

LEFT, TOP: The main door, with its simple design, is topped by a panel with palmette decoration protected by a projecting cornice supported by corbels.

LEFT, BOTTOM: An elaborate frieze of putti and garlands runs along the coping and frames the facade of the villa.

from the celebrated villa of Pliny. Peruzzi enjoyed immense prestige among his contemporaries—he was honored by burial in the Pantheon next to Raphael—but almost all the works that won him a place of honor among sixteenth-century Roman architects are no longer extant. Over the centuries the many facades he decorated have been mutilated or destroyed; the many stage sets he designed for the celebration of important events were ephemeral to begin with. For detailed accounts of his works we have only the descriptions that have survived from the past.

Villa Chigi is most famous for its fresco decorations, in particular those made by Raphael and his followers in the loggia connecting the two wings of the villa and overlooking the garden. Amid the bucolic simplicity of this setting the banker Chigi, known as "The Magnificent," held parties worthy of a prince's wealth. The garden loggia on the ground floor is decorated with scenes that present, far from any Christian reference, Agostino Chigi's horoscope, skillfully blending mythological figures with the emblems of the Zodiac following the ancient neoplatonic interpretation revised and brought back into fashion by the Tuscan humanist Marsilio Ficino. Like an elaborate good-luck charm, the ceiling was designed to protect Chigi with a favorable configuration of the sky, narrating the astral conjunc-

tions that had witnessed his birth in "the most extensive commemoration of a single individual in the High Renaissance" (S. J. Freedberg).

In the private rooms of this enchanting hide-away the leading artists of the Renaissance met. Their creations attest to Agostino

Chigi's cultural ambitions, and as banker to popes from Alexander VI to Leo X, he was the only man with the means to compete with Julius II for the services of the best artists available. These included Peruzzi, of course, and Raphael, who had been working for him since 1510

The famous garden loggia opens on the rear of the villa and once overlooked a vast garden, today in large part gone. In 1517 Raphael assembled his best students to work on the depiction of the story of Psyche and Cupid on the ceiling of the loggia. Giulio Romano, Giovanni da Udine, Giovan Francesco Penni, and Raffaello dal Colle worked following designs made by Raphael.

and who gave him two bronze medallions, today lost; there was also Sebastiano del Piombo, the great student of Giovanni Bellini, who came all the way from Venice in 1512 to paint the head of the giant Polyphemus. Sebastiano brought with him a sense of the great things happening in Venetian painting in the age of Giorgione (who had only recently died) and the young Titian. A year later, at the banker's request, Raphael painted a fresco of the *Triumph of Galatea* to complement Sebastiano's painting. Raphael's lively composition, in which the beautiful nymph Galatea is surrounded by frolicking sea creatures, is a work of masterful simplicity representative of the heights of Renaissance classicism; it is a perfect expression of that artist's poetic sensibilities. In 1517 Raphael and his best students painted the vault of the entrance loggia, orchestrating the events of Psyche and Cupid—and what background could have been more suitable for the banker's famous love affairs? While Giulio Romano frescoed the scenes with figures from *The Golden Ass* of Apuleius, Giovanni da Udine painted garlands of flowers and fruit. The explicitly erotic images of the gods and the sexual references hidden among the elegant festoons by Giovanni testify to the licentious habits of the first half of the sixteenth century. From the classical world of the ancient Romans Raphael and his students drew that type of decoration

The pagan fable of Psyche and Cupid is from Apuleius. Here, the three Graces listen to Cupid. The decorations were designed by Raphael and made by Giulio Romano, while the garlands of flowers and fruit were frescoed by Giovanni da Udine.

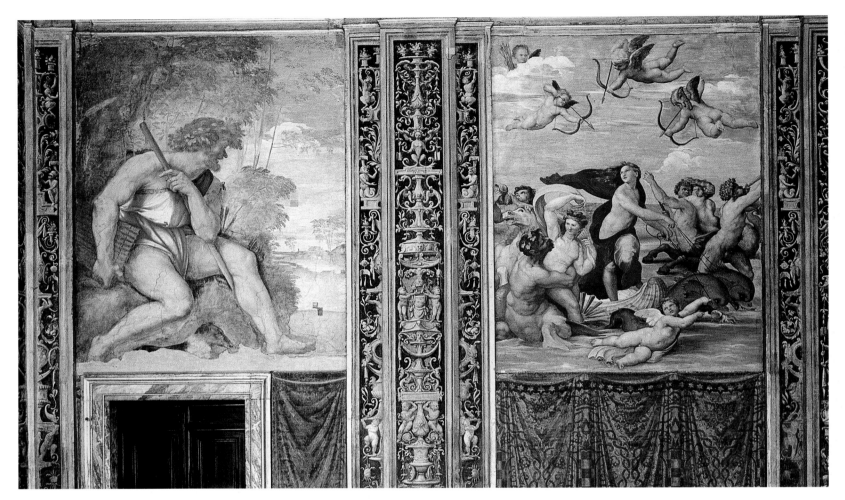

ABOVE: Sebastiano del Piombo arrived in Rome from Venice in 1511, bringing with him news of events taking place in Venetian painting. The next year, he painted the head of the giant Polyphemus in the garden loggia. In 1513 Raphael painted Galatea to one side, thus creating one of the masterpieces of Renaissance classicism.

LEFT: Agostino Chigi was among the most well-to-do and aggressive art patrons of his generation, and his villa became the meeting place for many leading artists of the Renaissance. The ceiling in the Sala di Galatea was decorated by Baldassare Peruzzi with the horoscope of Agostino Chigi, showing the planetary configuration at the time of the banker's birth, thus following a tradition revived by the humanist Marsilio Ficino.

OPPOSITE: Sebastiano del Piombo's depiction of the fall of Phaëthon is based on the tale as related in Ovid's *Metamorphoses,* but the dynamism of the tumbling figure recalls the works of Michelangelo. In fact, the young painter from the Veneto had only recently discovered Michelangelo, who was then working in the Sistine Chapel.

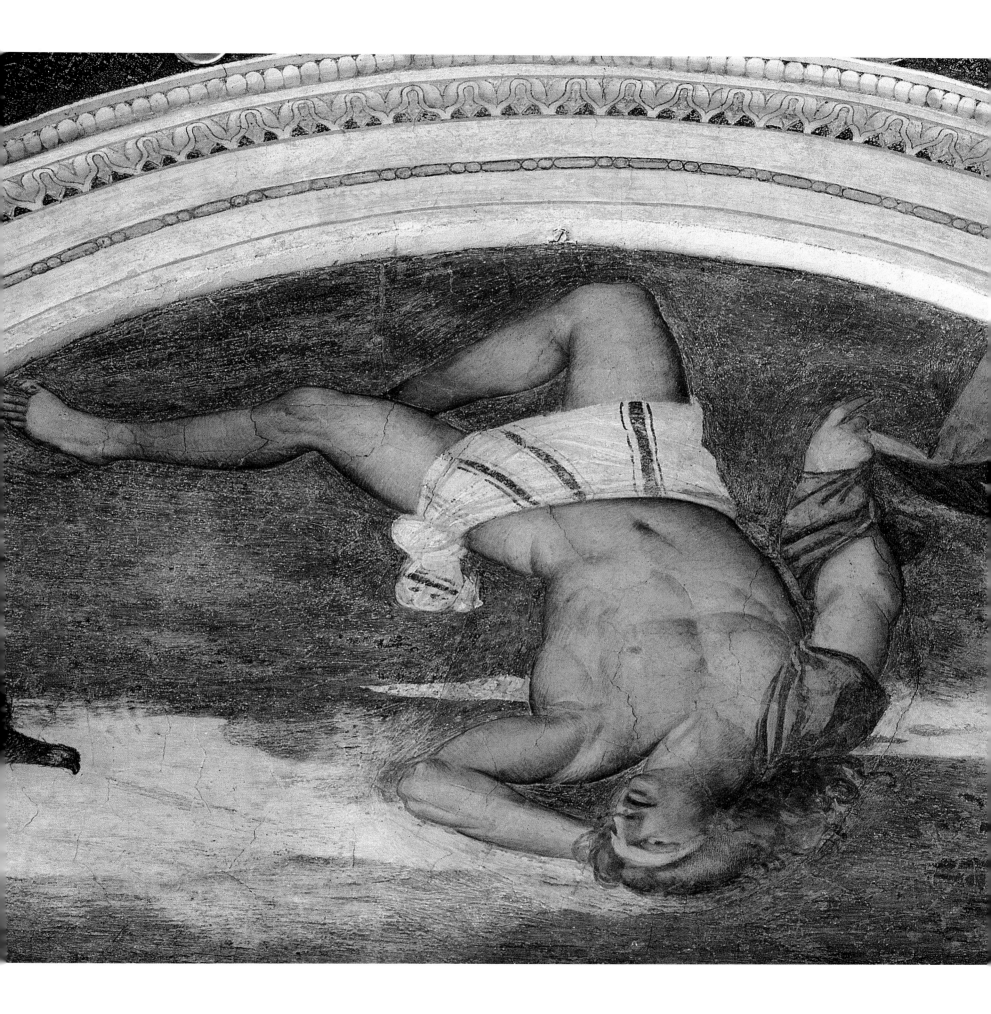

known as the grotesque (*alla grottesca*), since it was based on designs found in wall decorations in underground grottoes. The festoons, putti, shining candelabras, cornucopias, stela, and flowers represented the spirit of that society, displaying its sense of well-being and its carefree enjoyment of life.

On the second floor of the villa Peruzzi designed the Sala delle Prospettive, the decoration of which reflects the period's interest in illusionistic painting, including faux purple marble and faux balustrades opening onto cityscapes and views of the Roman countryside. This im-

portant decorative cycle, made between 1515 and 1517, stands out as a shining example of the surprising talents of this versatile artist. Adjacent to this salon is a bedroom, and for its decoration Chigi turned to the artist known to Vasari as Sodoma (Giovanni Antonio Bazzi), who came from Siena to paint such frescoes as *The Marriage of Alexander and Roxana*.

Sodoma finished these frescoes in 1518, the same year that Agostino Chigi married the mistress with whom he had been living for seven years and who ultimately bore him five children. The banker was notorious for his

personal appetites: he had begun his affair with the mistress after the deaths of his first wife and the famous courtesan Imperia. At the same time, he was known for his classical erudition—the source of Sodoma's frescoes was Lucian—and he founded a printing shop devoted to Greek authors.

Despite the central role that Agostino Chigi performed in its creation, the villa today bears—by an irony or perhaps a cruelty of fate—the name of the glorious Alessandro Farnese, who acquired it in 1579. By then, La Farnesina, as it is also known, had slowly fallen

Baldassare Peruzzi directed the decoration (1516–17) of the Sala delle Prospettive on the second floor of the villa, creating deceptive colonnades offering views of cities and landscapes following the style of illusionistic perspective of which he was a leading master. He was greatly admired in his lifetime for his state sets (now lost) and other ephemeral furnishings.

into decay, but the cardinal endeavored to revive it and had the fresco decorations finished in the Sala della Galatea. Gaspard Dughet added decorative landscapes of the Roman countryside following the style that became overwhelmingly popular following the arrival of Claude Lorrain. Reduced in size and disfigured, with much of the area of its magnificent garden stolen away, the villa today is but a shadow of its former self. Gone is the famous loggia open onto the Tiber where Agostino held banquets overlooking the trees and the river. At the end of each meal his guests tossed the precious table settings of silver and gold into the Tiber (where they were recovered after the guests had left, a net having been spread beneath the surface to catch them). Representative of a rich and cultured middle class, he wanted to create a place for

satisfying mind and body, far from every outward manifestation of power. His house was thus designed to express perfectly that desire for calm well-being that Leon Battista Alberti had described in his short work entitled *Villa;* at the villa, he wrote, you can "flee those uproars, those tumults, that tempest of the world, of the piazza, of the palace. You can hide yourself in the villa in order not to see the rascalities, the villainies, the quantity of wicked men that constantly passes before your eyes in the city." That spirit still emanates from what remains of this magic place.

Agostino Chigi's bedroom is decorated with *The Marriage of Alexander and Roxana* and *The Young Macedonian Taming Bucephalus,* subjects taken from Lucian. Giovanni Antonio Bazzi, the artist known as Sodoma, made this decorative cycle between 1516 and 1518. The quality of the central part of the fresco, the part showing the taming of Bucephalus, is so inferior to the rest of the fresco that art historians believe this part of the wall to be originally occupied by the banker's bed, and thus entrusted to one of Bazzi's assistants.

Villa Madama

The Villa Madama, designed by Raphael for Cardinal Giulio de' Medici and celebrated as one of the first modern re-creations of a Roman country villa—and, as such, one of the earliest expressions of the impact of classicism—has suffered a fate fully as harsh and tormented as that of its original owner. When he was cardinal in the court of his cousin Leo X, Giulio de' Medici led a care-free existence as a member of the restricted and erudite circle around that great Renaissance pope; all this changed after he was himself elected pope as Clement VII (1523–34) and found himself forced to witness firsthand the break-up of the humanist dream and the culminating moment of that collapse, the ferocious sack of Rome in 1527 at the hands of the mercenary troops of Charles V. Originally planned as a work without equal, capable of handing on to posterity the towering grandeur of the Medici family, the villa has barely survived and no longer even bears a Medici name.

The planning of the villa dates to the golden period of the youth of Giulio de' Medici, whose training and education took place in the

The villa that Cardinal Giuliano de' Medici commissioned Raphael to design in 1518 remained unfinished, and later work by Guilio Romano and Antonio Sangallo did not respect the original designs. The main facade stands on a semicircular court that was supposed to be preceded by a series of terraces. A large garden was supposed to surround the villa, which the cardinal hoped would be the most luxurious in Rome, a revival of the true spirit of the villas of antiquity.

heart of the classical ideals of the Renaissance. Raphael, the artist who most closely expressed those ideals, conceived the plan as a grandiose response to the beauties of classical antiquity, a creation full of pleasures and surprises in accordance with the cardinal's wishes to "erect a palace furnished with convenient rooms, loggias, gardens, fountains, woods, and other things of beauty," as Vasari reports. The actual building of the villa, however, proved sadly unfortunate, interrupted first by the death of the great master in 1520; then by the death of Pope Leo X in 1521 and the cardinal's two-year stay in Florence during the reign of Pope Adrian VI; and finally by the sack in 1527, which led to the mutilation of the villa's appearance. Thus this ambitious project, meant to represent the culmination of Raphael's theories as an architect, was destined to remain in the incomplete state it had reached just before 1527.

After taking the place of Bramante as first architect of the pope in 1514, Raphael began receiving a great many commissions and was forced to make increasing use of his team of assistants, chief among them Giulio Romano. Work on the villa began under Raphael's direct supervision in the last months of 1518; but as with other commissions, he was soon joined by his pupils. The humanistic architects of the period were obsessed by the great villas of antiquity, and they sought

to evoke them in modern works. In a recently discovered letter, Raphael himself provides a detailed description of this complex work, in which he planned to bring to life the spirit of the villas of ancient Rome. Raphael envisioned a series of rooms, at different levels extending

accommodations were nearby to delight them and meet their every need, whether physical or spiritual. The villa's layout included rooms designed, by their orientation, to serve certain purposes according to the season, some offering relief from summer heat, others provid-

across the hillside down to the river, that would together form a large complex. In terms of both their size and their sequence, these rooms were designed for large-scale receptions, splendid celebrations for foreign diplomats arriving in Rome by way of the Milvian Bridge, which until the first century before Christ had been the city's main entrance. Guests were to be welcomed at a garden terrace with a semicircular theater, based on ancient Roman theaters. Fish ponds, stables with space for up to four hundred horses, and all

ing shelter in the winter, all in imitation of the ancient models so familiar to Raphael, such as Hadrian's villa and the grottoes of Tivoli.

A very general sense of Raphael's original design plan can be gleaned from surviving documents, but the great many changes made during the course of the actual construction work created a gulf between the original plan and the final creation. The overall principles of monumental harmony and the references to the architecture of Bramante leave no doubts concerning what Raphael

The magnificent loggia is sure proof of the presence of Raphael and his leading students. Divided in three bays and closed over by barrel vaults, it is skillfully articulated following complex classical harmonies and is one of Raphael's greatest achievements in the field of architecture.

had in mind for most of the structure. The original plans are reflected in a dozen preparatory sketches; but here, too, many changes were made during the complex phase of actually building the structure. Raphael himself made the fish pond—it was left unfinished—and he probably intended to cover it with sculptural decoration and surround it with plays of water from fountains. Interrupted by the master's death, the work was continued by Raphael's students Antonio da Sangallo, Giovanni da Udine, and Giulio Romano. Giovanni da Udine modeled the white stucco reliefs of the walls based on "ruins in Titus's palace." His presence is documented by inscriptions on the decorated pilasters bearing his name and the date 1525. Giulio Romano probably initially replaced Raphael in the direction of the work. He was full of enthusiasm for the villa and for the idea behind it—that of creating an evocation of the rustic villas of the past. In fact, he depicted the villa in an incomplete phase, still surrounded by scaffolding, in his fresco of the battle near Ponte Molle in the Vatican Stanze. Giulio Romano was drawn to the odd and eccentric, and his creations probably evoked in the spectator the same sense of uncertainty as do those he made in Mantua's Palazzo Tè. His particular style can also be seen in the stuccoes of the exedra and in the central dome of the great hall, covered with cupids, garlands,

candelabras, and winged victories. In a letter written to Bishop Maffei, who was overseeing the work, Giuliano de' Medici discussed the themes he preferred in pictorial decoration. He suggested opting for well-known pagan fables, for the presentation of clear, easily comprehensible narra-

very little remains of the giant with infants and satyrs playing about him. The remaining decorations of the vault were supposed to be designed by Giovanni da Udine and Baldassare Peruzzi. The bishop's letters back to Giuliano mention frequent disputes over the division of

BELOW: The decoration of the loggia was executed by Giulio Romano and Giovanni da Udine, but the stuccoes, paintings, and grotesques follow a decorative program that was worked out by Raphael, at least in its general lines, given their associations with the loggias in the Vatican and in the Chigi Chapel. The central vault shows the four seasons in stucco and frescoes, with mythological scenes.

tions. The famous fresco of Polyphemus that Giulio Romano painted in the lunette is certainly in keeping with his patron's carefree taste and is inspired by a fable from Ovid. Unfortunately the frescoes are now in a poor state of preservation, and

the work and refer to Giulio Romano and Giovanni da Udine as "a pair of lunatics."

Antonio da Sangallo the Younger actively participated in the creation of the villa, most probably performing the role of technical adviser, much as he had in St. Peter's,

OPPOSITE: The coat of arms of Cardinal Giuliano de' Medici appears at the center of the rectangle in the middle of the vault of the large hall. It is flanked by images of the Sun and the Moon; around this are decorative motifs that connect the cardinal's emblems to elements taken from the classical repertory of images.

where he had served as adviser alongwide Raphael. He is credited with a long series of preliminary studies, as well as with the creation of the courtyard, with its circular layout and niche decoration. In all likelihood, it was also Sangallo the Younger who designed the Vitruvian theater.

Work on the villa was interrupted by the death of Leo X. Cardinal Giulio de' Medici was away from Rome, primarily in Florence, during the period just before his nomination to the papacy, in November 1523, but he turned his attention to the villa again as soon as he got

back. This is confirmed by the diaries of Marino Sanuto, who records that Giulio went horseback riding there on the very day of his election. Not long afterward, during the sack of Rome in 1527, the mercenary soldiers eager to hang Clement VII destroyed much of the villa. The magnificent loggia, its monumental bays opening onto the garden, still stands.

Having survived the threat to his life, the pope soon arranged two astute marriages: that of his niece Catherine de' Medici to the second-born son of the king of France and that of Alessandro de' Medici

to Margaret, known as Madama, the illegitimate daughter of Emperor Charles V. It is for this young woman, although she made no contribution to it, that the villa is named. Thus what was meant to be the most celebrated Roman villa of the sixteenth century was destined to become a simple hayloft. Never completed, devastated, and then restored, the villa survives as a pale shadow of its original plans.

During this century, the architect Marcello Piacentini has undertaken large-scale restoration work, altering the villa's original arrangement.

The frieze by Giulio Romano in the Sala del Fregio presents dancing girls along with animals and cupids. The vaulted ceiling is framed by an inclined band of decoration divided in sections by elegant fretwork and presenting mythological fables.

Villa Giulia

In 1550, a year of jubilee, Cardinal Giovanni Maria del Monte was elected pope as Julius III (1550–55). He owed his election to the political acumen he had demonstrated in negotiations with Charles V and the Holy Roman Empire. His ascension to the papal seat led to a minor revival of Renaissance spirit, a rekindling of archaeological and aesthetic taste. After careful consideration, he brought a brief suspension to the tormented debates caused by the Council of Trent, thus giving the city a respite during which he dedicated his energies to the realization of a dream. It was during those years and in that spirit that he decided to transform an overgrown farm outside the city walls into a magnificent country villa, and he put so much passion into his plans for the villa that to the chronicler Onofrio Panvinio it seemed the pope was driving himself crazy "for those gardens." Julius III began work on his ambitious projects right away. He directed most of his efforts to holdings that his family had assembled in the area between the Tiber and the slope of Monte Valentino, today the hill of Parioli, holdings that

LEFT AND BELOW: The stern facade designed by Giacomo da Vignola contrasts with the broad garden front, the semicircular shape of which affects the internal shape of the building.

OPPOSITE: The far wall of the courtyard is decorated with stucco embellishments. A loggia leads to the nymphaeum, a work by Bartolomeo Ammanati, whose signature appears on the last pilaster to the right.

had been steadily extended, coming to include, aside from numerous farms and vineyards, the holy burial place of Sant'Andrea.

From the very beginning, three well-known architects —Ammanati, Vasari, and Vignola—gravitated around the pope, responding to the whims of this authoritarian patron and sharing and exchanging ideas in such a complex arrangement that their contributions can no longer be easily distinguished. The great Michelangelo himself is mentioned in a Florentine document according to which "nothing was done without the advice of Buonarroti." Vasari gives himself credit for being "the first to plan the villa" and for making the designs "according to the pope's ideas," although he admits the actual work was carried out by others. In fact, direction of the work was entrusted to the Bolognese painter Prospero Fontana (1512–1597), whom the pope had met in 1534 when he was still cardinal and serving as papal legate in Bologna. Various letters he wrote in that period reveal that even then he was thinking about the potential of the villa. As early as 1539 he discusses both the importance of exploiting agricultural possibilities and the intellectual pleasures that might be enjoyed in such an ideal setting.

The absence of an overall plan and the mingling of so many different artists in the effort makes it difficult to assess the history of the villa's

construction. We do know, however, that Giacomo da Vignola (1507–1573) eventually became Julius III's favorite architect. It was Vignola who began work on the construction of a simple palace whose somber walls concealed the delights of a worldly court. The Tridentine

dictates may have sought to impose new standards, but Julius III, offspring of the Renaissance, wished to surround himself with the kind of earthly and luxurious pleasures represented by his suburban home, which came to take up his energies, leaving but few for his city residence,

Water from the Acqua Vergine aqueduct was channeled into the scenic nymphaeum and then directed into splashing fountains, creating a "theater of water." Antique marbles, finely hammered metals, and statues from the collection of Julius III add to the setting. The loggias are supported by herm-caryatids, with statues of river gods against the back walls.

PAGES 264–265: Direction of the villa's painted decoration was entrusted entirely to the brothers Federico and Taddeo Zuccaro, who, together with their workshop assistants, decorated the vaults and friezes with mythological figures. The open gallery of the courtyard is covered with plant decoration in imitation of a pergola.

located in a palace near the Campus Martius. Every day he acquired antique statues to install somewhere in his villa.

Work on the villa was completed in only two years. Its exterior presents a face in keeping with the times, in full conformity with the strict rules of decorum; its interior is a creation of rich fantasy, conducive to the celebration of antique splendors hidden by a high wall, a *hortus conclusis* in which to indulge, far from the eyes of the world, the personal expressions of an intense antiquarian passion.

The courtyard, enclosed by a broad semicircular portico, provided the original spatial layout for the main body of the villa. The ground floor was frescoed by the celebrated workshop directed by Taddeo Zuccaro. In the Sala dei Sette Colli, this artist painted scenes following the nascent style of landscape painting, while the decorations were characterized in general by an excellent Raphael-like style and by playful references to the classical. The artists who worked on the second-floor Stanza delle Quattro Stagioni and Stanza delle Arti Liberali certainly belonged to the sphere of the Zuccaro brothers, the principal heirs of the style of decoration popularized by Perino del Vaga, but the identification of individual artists is made difficult by the homogeneous pictorial elegance. Another courtyard led from the villa to the theatrical nymphaeum, made by Ammanati, a lively

and joyous setting with walls originally covered by precious marbles, hammered metals, and an opulent profusion of gold and stuccoes that descended all the way to the grotto below, forming an exuberant "water theater." This was the center of the villa, and also its most heavily decorated spot. Its creation had been part of the earliest plans, as indicated by a document from 1552 that records the presentation of a model for the fountain to the pope. To provide water for this elegant aquatic complex, Julius III commissioned a large-scale project designed to bring water from the Acqua Vergine aqueduct right up to the steps of the villa. The loggia of the nymphaeum was completed by the end of 1553. That same year Vasari was commissioned to make sketches with mythological scenes for the wall decorations. The appearance of the complex today has been altered by large-scale restoration work performed in the eighteenth century.

The pope personally oversaw the project in all its various details, even choosing the species of fruit tree to be used. In fact, his obsession with the tiniest details became common knowledge. Over a period of five years, this immense property, which originally covered all the hills from the Aurelian walls to the Milvian Bridge, took form. The site was once covered with smaller structures that no longer exist. The Tempieto designed by

Vignola, today bordered by Via Flaminia, was once buried in a dense forest of laurels. Nearby stood three villas. A spacious garden surrounded the main building, its area strewn with ancient relics and inscriptions, while the park was designed with "places for repose and tables

in the shade or most commodious loggias of greenery or of masonry," according to Ammanati's writings.

Quick-tempered and somewhat blunt, Julius III attracted more than his share of enemies, and after his death, in 1555, his beloved

villa was mercilessly sacked. The pope's home was stripped of furnishings, its aviaries were emptied, statues stolen, bubbling fountains shut off. Over the centuries, it became a storage dump for agricultural implements.

Now open to the public as the seat of an Etruscan

museum, the Villa Giulia has, following restoration of those portions that survived all of time's ravages, a new dignity. But its appearance for the most part does not convey the grandiose plans of the man who first envisioned it.

Today the villa is a museum housing a collection of pre-Roman antiquities, in particular an important collection of Etruscan works.

Villa Medici

From its very beginning, the Villa Medici was meant to be marvelous; it was a home built to enchant and to astonish. Cardinal Giovanni Ricci of Montepulciano (1497–1574), a wealthy and powerful Tuscan, put antique sculptures and parrots, slaves and Moors within its walls, bringing splendor and life back to places imbued with classical memories. Such classical allusions were appropriate for the Pincian Hill in the northeastern area of the city, the site of the celebrated villa of Lucullus, which with the passing of the centuries had fallen into ruin, untended and abandoned. A drawing by Pirro Ligorio suggests some of its splendor. It stood in the area of the convent of Trinità dei Monti and probably occupied terraces set along the slope of the Pincian Hill. A few remains of this grandiose villa, built with great style and on a large scale, are still visible in the underground areas of the convent.

Immediately after acquiring a small holding from the Crescenzi family, Cardinal Ricci called on his faithful architect, Nanni di Baccio Bigio (c. 1512–1568), who

OPPOSITE: The Villa Medici's garden facade was built for the powerful and cultured Cardinal Giovanni Ricci of Montepulciano by Annibale Lippi. Its plaster walls are inlaid with ancient bas-reliefs, testimony to the cardinal's great passion for archaeological relics. The pleasing facade with the Serlian-motif loggia at the center is flanked by two projecting structures topped by small towers. The profusion of stone tablets, busts, and ancient bas-reliefs was later emulated at Villa Borghese.

ABOVE: This window is flanked on the left by a fragment with a scene of Diana and Apollo and on the right by a scene with a mythological figure kneeling before a winged Eros.

had already worked for him on a Vatican apartment and in his palace in Via Giulia. A Florentine by birth, Nanni followed the Roman tradition of Antonio da Sangallo, to which he added his own exceptional technical skills, but he died in 1568, before seeing the work to its conclusion. It was then taken up by Giacomo della Porta, a student of Michelangelo who had become one of the most esteemed artists of the period and who made many churches and fountains, contributing much to creating the sixteenth-century face of Rome.

The loggia of the palace was certainly designed by this artist, as is confirmed by the capitals, which match those he made alongside Michelangelo for the Palazzo dei Conservatori. At the same time, the cardinal enlarged the garden by acquiring surrounding plots of land, and he filled the area with magnificent relics, including several bas-reliefs from the Ara Pacis that remained on the site for more than two centuries.

Giovanni Ricci died in 1574, and two years later the villa passed into the hands of that period's richest and most powerful cardinal, Ferdinando de' Medici, fifth son of Grand Duke of Tuscany Cosimo I. The Medici's official architect, Bartolomeo Ammanati, was summoned to adapt the central body of the villa, to beautify the garden, and in general to add splendor and elegance to this new Medici property. Like most powerful

The sides of the two flights of the main stairs were originally decorated with lions, one from the Roman age and the other made by Flaminio Vacca between 1570 and 1590; these have been replaced by marble copies. A replica of the *Mercury* by Giambologna recalls the magnificent collection of sculptural pieces that were originally spread throughout the villa, but which were moved to Florence during the eighteenth century by the villa's later owner, Grand Duke Cosimo III. The works were put on display at the Loggia dei Lanzi.

men of his time, Ferdinando was fond of hunting, games, and classical antiquity, probably in that order, since in 1578 a group of cardinals lamented that he was "not attending to state matters, but is continually hunting."

Running beneath the coat of arms of the cardinal and giving majesty to the loggia was a large Serlian motif, based on the designs of Sebastiano Serlio, the Italian architect, theorist, and painter whose decorative motifs were adopted throughout Europe. Also dating to this period is the creation of the long gallery built to house the extraordinary collection of ancient statues that the cardinal collected, competing in these efforts with the Farnese and Este families. The collection of busts and bas-reliefs that Ferdinando put together came to be considered among the city's most exquisite, inferior only to those of the pope and the Farnese. He bought the collection of the Del Bufalo family and, even more important, that of the Della Valle family. This collection came to constitute the nucleus of the Uffizi Gallery's ancient sculptures. It was then, too, that the garden was given the magnificence it still possesses. Ammanati designed the beautiful spiral stairway and enlarged the vestibule on the ground floor to create a truly monumental entrance way. Ancient columns made of polychrome marble were set up in the great hall leading to the loggia. Statuary groups

Cardinal Ricci of Montepulciano devoted much time and care to the villa's garden, decorating it with a wealth of ancient sculptures and filling it with exotic plants, parrots, and other curiosities, seeking thereby to re-create the spirit of the villa of Lucullus, which stood on the same site in the Roman age. He commissioned the architect Bartolomeo Ammanati to embellish the garden, which was then used as a setting for statuary, such as the celebrated Medici Vase and the Sabine women from Trajan's forum, works that today are in the Uffizi.

were put in place everywhere. These included the famous Medici vase, the Sabine women from Trajan's forum, the *Venus de' Medici*, the *Dacians*, and the *Knife-grinder*. The cardinal showed an equal passion for painting, and his collection included a *Madonna* by Raphael and numerous works by Andrea del Sarto, Pontormo, Salviati, and others.

The cardinal was in the habit of meeting his lover, Clelia Farnese, atop one of the ancient towers in the nearby Aurelian walls. By then, however, the permissive attitudes of the late Renaissance were being swept away by the stern dictates of the Counter Reformation, and Ferdinando, in order to avoid prying eyes, had a small apartment built there. It was decorated to create a kind of pavilion. Its vaults were frescoed by Jacopo Zucchi with plant and animal motifs. A window gave a view of the Roman countryside. A pergola covered with numerous painted birds

ABOVE: The loggia connects to a large vaulted atrium; the niches in the atrium's walls once held objects from the sculpture collection. The windows over the doors give light to the vestibule, as do two smaller openings in the cornice just beneath the ceiling. The cornice itself is supported by pilasters decorated with Ionic capitals.

OPPOSITE: The villa's main staircase, opposite the main entrance, has several stretches with spiral stairways (the niche in the background contains an ancient statue).

offered both shelter and pleasure. There can be no doubt that the cardinal sensed the need to flee the new Tridentine reforms. Even a collection of antiquities was no longer looked upon with such a benevolent eye, and under the papacy of Pius V, those who found joy in acquiring pagan works began to be looked on with disapproval. Ferdinando de' Medici still belonged to the world of the Renaissance, but it was a world in decline. The cardinal's biographer, Pietro Usibaldi, wrote that the cardinal "certainly did not lack an inclination for the lascivious," but he also recalled that the cardinal had a true love for nature, following in this the passions of his father, Cosimo I, who was responsible for the creation of the botanical gardens of Pisa and Florence. Much like Zucchi's frescoes, the Villa Medici was full of rare species of plant and animal. The animals included some quite unusual beasts. People wrote of spotting ostriches among the garden plants, a tiger and a lion were on hand, even a bear chained to a post in the yard.

In 1587, when, as heir, Ferdinando de' Medici became in his turn grand duke, he left Rome for Florence. It was there that he celebrated his marriage to Christine of Lorraine, granddaughter of Queen Catherine de' Medici. The villa then began a slow decline into neglect. Ferdinando's son Carlo de' Medici preferred life in Florence to life at the Roman villa, and

other successors simply lost interest. During the seventeenth century work on the villa was limited to what was absolutely necessary. Thus began the dark years that ended with the transfer of the painting collection to the Pitti palace in Florence under Grand Duke Cosimo III. He

Ferdinando de' Medici had the small pavilion that stands on a stretch of the Aurelian walls built as a private spot for rendezvous with his lover, Clelia Farnese. It is decorated with plant and animal motifs by the Tuscan painter Jacopo Zucchi; its spirit of lively curiosity in the things of the natural world reflects the pagan elegance of the late Renaissance. The villa's garden was planted with exotic species of plants; it was also a kind of zoo, with such unusual animals as tiger, lion, and bear chained to the post, along with various birds, including ostriches.

also had it in mind to eliminate the magnificent loggia and replace it with a closed salon, but that plan, fortunately, was not carried out. Gian Gastone, the last Medici, undertook restoration work to consolidate the villa, but at his death, in 1737, ownership passed to the house of Lorraine. The archaeological collection was moved to Florence in 1770. When the Academy of France decided to move its headquarters from Palazzo Mancini on the Via del Corso to the Pincian Hill, a new period of glory began for the magnificent home.

It was during the reign of Louis XIV that the habit of seeking artists in Italy began to wane and the supremacy that Italian artists had so long enjoyed in foreign courts began to weaken. One of the most emblematic events in this regard involved the great sculptor and architect Bernini, whom Louis XIV called to Paris to finish designing the Louvre only to reject his proposed plans. French artists grew more sure of themselves, and hostility toward Italian painting increased. It was not by chance that all of the decoration of Versailles was done by painters from the northern side of the Alps. In 1666, with the full support of the Sun King himself, the decision was made to create a French academy in Rome to make it possible for French art students to share the great opportunity Italian students had to study firsthand the masterpieces of the past.

Colbert, Le Brun, and Bernini provided early impetus to the Académie de France, which holds competitions and then rewards the winners with the opportunity to live and study in Rome. The winners are thus given the opportunity to concentrate their efforts on making copies of sculpture

The Camera Turca was decorated under the guidance of Horace Vernet, who served as director of the Académie de France from 1828 to 1834; it is covered by Moorish majolica tiles and its vault is painted with a geometric Arabic motif. The villa's sixteenth-century walls were once hung with the painting collection, but those works are now in the Uffizi. The villa has but few fresco decorations. The painter Balthus served as director of the academy from 1961 to 1977 and supervised restoration of the villa.

and paintings. The French Revolution reduced the activity of the academy. In fact, several years began during which the academy's main building in Palazzo Mancini on the Via del Corso was ransacked and otherwise damaged by young counter-revolutionaries. The academy came back to life during the period of the Consulate, at which time the decision was made to move the main building to the Villa Medici on the Pincian Hill. An important period thus began for both the villa and the academy. Large-scale construction projects were undertaken, with classrooms and apartments set up in the gardens; and new areas of study, including music and engraving, were added to those already covered by the academy. The painters who stayed at the villa during the nineteenth century included Ingres, Flandrin, and Cabanel; among the sculptors were Carpeaux and David d'Angers; among the musicians were Berlioz, Massenet, Charpentier, and Debussy. The academy entered a period of renewed vitality following the Second World War, thanks in part to the efforts of André Malraux, then France's minister of cultural affairs. A project was launched to restore the villa to its sixteenth-century state, and copies were made of the most famous ancient statuary groups, which were then used to decorate the loggia and garden. In 1961, Malraux nominated the painter Balthus to be director general, and

under Balthus further initiatives were undertaken, including the addition of new areas of study, such as film-making and photography, and the organization of exhibitions and concerts. Since then this magnificent setting has been the stage for a revival of the very same Renaissance spirit of love and support of the arts that inspired Giovanni Ricci of Montepulciano and Ferdinando de' Medici to build the villa in the first place.

At the center of the elaborate ceiling in the Camera delle Muse is this presentation with Terpsichore, Jupiter, and Minerva, painted by Jacopo Zucchi around 1580. This is one of a series of paintings made for Ferdinando de' Medici that share complex allusions, blending motifs from astrology, mythology, and esoteric episodes referring to the political ambitions of the young cardinal, who was constantly involved in heated dynastic struggles.

Villa Borghese

In 1605, when Camillo Borghese, member of an aristocratic Roman family with Sienese origins, was elected pope as Paul V (1605–21), the way was opened for a new era in patronage of the arts, one dominated by a return of gaiety and indulgence. Heir, together with his brothers, to an old piece of property at the Muro Torto, he began buying up the surrounding lots, eventually coming into possession of the extraordinary park that is still without equal in Rome in terms of size and grandeur.

Flaminio Ponzio (1560–1613) was commissioned to design the villa, which the pope and his ambitious nephew Scipione Caffarelli Borghese intended to use for splendid banquets. The Dutch architect and cabinetmaker Giovanni Vasanzio (Jan, or Giovanni, van Santen; ca. 1550–1621), the family's favorite artist and the designer of a palace on the Quirinal, was commissioned to transform the vast, uncultivated grounds into a delightful garden spread with niches and statues. Work on the rectangular palace and its two towers was far along, although not yet finished, when Ponzio died, in 1613.

Work on the Casino dell'Uccelliera, following a design by Girolamo Rainaldi, began in 1617 and ended in 1619, at which time the Venetian copper wire used for the cages was paid for. The exterior of the small building was decorated with numerous stuccoworks, sculptures, and antique polychrome marbles, and it faced onto a secret walled garden.

Vasanzio took over direction of the work, completing the exterior decoration of the building, which was composed entirely of archaeological relics from the collections of the pope and Scipione as if to announce to visitors the building's true nature as a private museum. The two powerful men were most interested in creating an appropriate setting for their magnificent collection of antiquities, which they assembled with unabated fervor. The decision to use sculpture framed by stuccowork as

decoration for the facade, in keeping with the style employed earlier for the Villa Medici, permitted the use of 70 busts, 43 statues, and 144 bas-reliefs, as indicated by a painting of 1636 by Johan Wilhelm Bauer. Most of the work on the palace had been completed when Vazanzio died in 1621; his place was then taken by Girolamo Rainaldi. The planting of the garden was entrusted to the well-known gardener Domenico Savino of Montepulciano. Rainaldi designed several smaller structures for the

Scipione Borghese commissioned Giovanni Lanfranco for the fresco *The Gods in Council with Jupiter* on the ceiling of the loggia that opens on the *piano nobile* of the Casino. Lanfranco left the painting unfinished, and Domenico Corvi was summoned to complete it in 1782.

OPPOSITE: Antonello da Messina, *Portrait of a Man*, c. 1474–75.

garden, including the Uccelliera, topped by a spire of copper wire, the similar building known as the Meridiana because of its sundial, and also two theaters that are today largely destroyed. Around this time (1620–25), Scipione commissioned Giovanni Lanfranco to make a large ceiling fresco in the villa of the *Gods of Olympus*, which for many years was the largest and most ambitiously carried-out ceiling fresco in Rome.

From its very beginning, the palace built by the two leading members of the Borghese family was meant to house the family's archaeological collection, particularly the pieces assembled by Scipione, who in 1607 had acquired a collection of 278 statues from the Ceuli family of bankers and then two years later had bought the collection of the sculptor Giovanni Battista della Porta. Unfortunately, no works from this original collection remain in the villa today. The Borghese family married into Napoleon's family and gave France in 1807 the so-called Borghese nucleus of the Louvre. The villa that Scipione desired was radically modified during the eighteenth century, but notary documents, period engravings, and the contemporary descriptions prepared by the villa's curator Jacomo Manili permit a detailed re-creation of the original layout. The rolling grounds had been divided into three areas, two of which were used for

versions of what contemporary style called "sylvan woods," and the third of which was put to agricultural uses. The first of the three areas was composed of geometric beds marked off by pathways and hedges of boxwood modeled according to antique designs for topiary

art. The second area, called the secret garden, was used for the cultivation of flowers. This was the area with the birdcage house and the rabbit hutch along with a deer park. Fountains fed by water from the Acqua Felice aqueduct, a privilege accorded

This Roman statue illustrating *Youth and the Dolphin* dates to the Antonine period and most likely adorned a fountain.

OPPOSITE: Antonio Canova's *Pauline*, dated 1805, presents Napoleon's sister, Pauline, striking a pose as Venus. One of the most famous works of neoclassicism, it has been acclaimed as a masterpiece since the day it was unveiled, and was exalted by Flaubert as a symbol of beauty. In the background is a perspective view by Giovan Battista Marchetti.

the villa by Paul V in 1617, were spread throughout the park. Flaminio Ponzio had drawn up the plans for the large Italian-style garden himself, as can be seen on a contemporary engraving.

The celebrated painting collection that is the basis of today's museum dates to the

BELOW: Tiziano Vecellio, *Sacred Love and Profane Love*, 1514. The work was done for Nicolo Aurelio, secretary for Venice's Council of Ten.

OPPOSITE: Raphael Sanzio, *Deposition*, 1507. Commissioned by Atalanta Baglioni in memory of his dead son, the painting was removed from the Church of Perugia in 1608 on the orders of Scipione Borghese, causing an uprising among the people.

early years of the seventeenth century. Camillo and Scipione dedicated a large portion of their immense wealth to the construction of chapels and monuments. Enormous volumes of archival documents attest to the expenses sustained by the rich cardinal, who created the core of the collection. Although notorious for the "mediocrity of his knowledge and life given over to pleasures and pastimes," the pope's nephew had an obsessive urge to collect works of art and was capable of even unscrupulous acts to possess them. When he could not buy them, he was not above "requisitioning"

PAGE 290: Gian Lorenzo Bernini made his *David* in 1619, early in his career as a sculptor, presenting himself in the figure of David. Bernini made the statue for his patron, Scipione Borghese, who valued its dynamism and expressive intensity.

PAGE 291: *The Rape of Persephone*, another early work of Gian Lorenzo Bernini for Scipione Borghese, is based on the myth of Persephone, who was carried off by Pluto with the assistance of his three-headed dog, Cerberus.

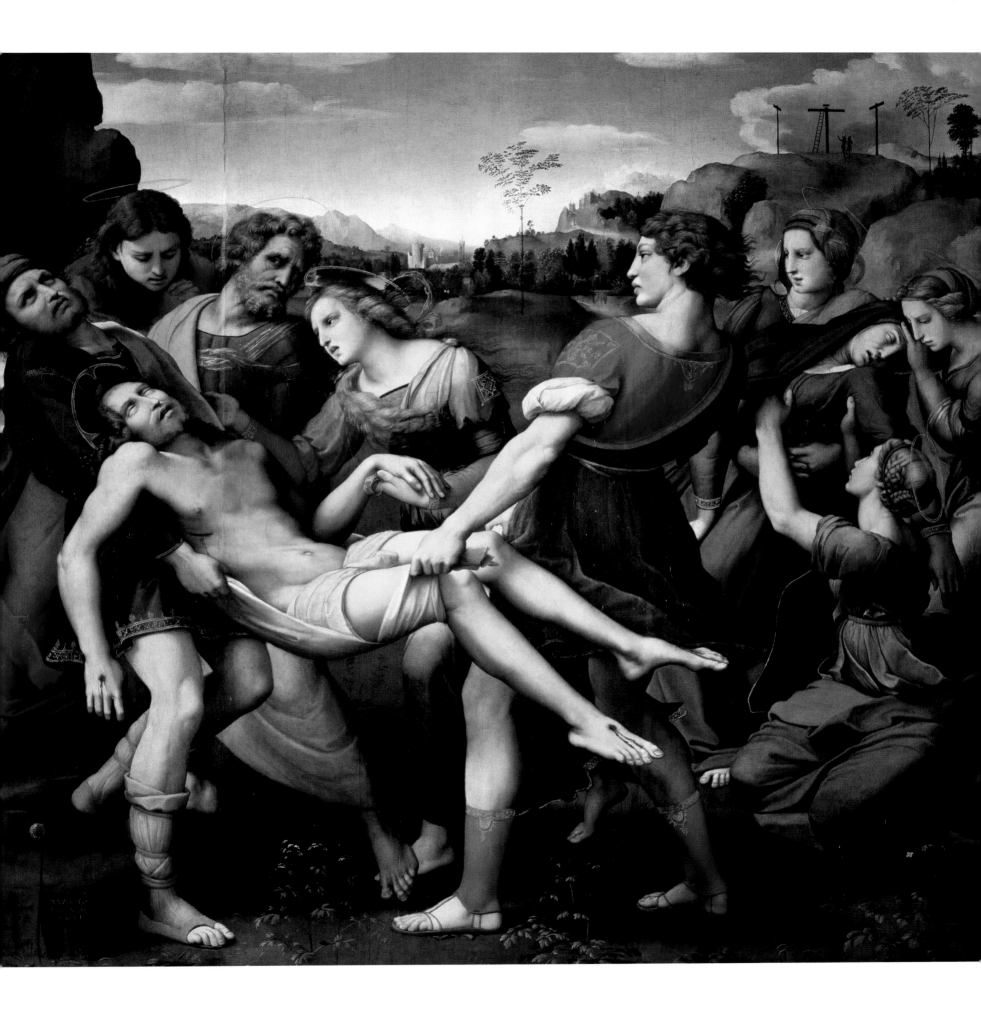

them. This was the method he employed to confiscate 105 canvases from the unfortunate Cavaliere d'Arpino, who had fallen on hard times after the death of his protector, Pope Clement VII. The works included several by the young Caravaggio. Similarly, at his command, the famous *Deposition* by Raphael was stolen away at night from the Church of San Francesco in Perugia. Paolo Borghese's marriage to Olimpia Aldobrandini brought into the family many other works of exceptional interest. By the end of the seventeenth century the painting collection had reached an incomparable size.

At Scipione's death, in 1633, the trustee overseeing the estate gave the entire property as inheritance to a cousin, Marcantonio II. In these years the palace was brought to a stage of thorough completion, as can be seen in the painting by Bauer, in which the palace has a dramatic double stairway, which was removed in the eighteenth century. Building work was later brought to a halt, for the Aldobrandini branch of the family was far more interested in tending to its farms and horses. This state of artistic languor was broken two centuries later under Marcantonio IV, with new works directed by the architect Antonio Asprucci, who radically changed the interior decoration of the villa, giving it the appearance it has today. This period of the last years of the eigh-

teenth century saw the triumph of the neoclassical style with its attendant thirst for all things archaeological. The true apex of this search for ideal nobility is represented by the sublime stateliness of Antonio Canova's marble sculpture of Pauline Borghese as Venus, a work that seems

BELOW: Dosso Dossi, *Maga Circe*, or *Melissa*, 1525. The painting was probably part of the collection of Scipione Borghese through Enzo Bentivoglio, who in 1608 gave his grandson diverse paintings from Ferrara from his father.

OPPOSITE: The sculpture *Aeneas and Anchises* is the work of Pietro Bernini, father of Gian Lorenzo.

LEFT: The Sala Egizia is named for the outstanding collection of Egyptian sculptures that were displayed there until being removed during the Napoleonic period; today they are in the Louvre. At the center of the room is a Roman statue of a youth and a dolphin, which dates to the Antonine period and probably once decorated a fountain. The images based on the history of ancient Egypt that decorate the walls are by Giovan Battista Marchetti and Tommaso Conca.

emblematic of the decorations in the rooms. The amazing discoveries of Pompeii and Herculaneum, which led Goethe to exclaim, "No catastrophe has ever been the source of greater pleasure for the rest of mankind as the one that buried these two cities," provided the inspiration for that cold, crystalline beauty. Each room had particular features, beginning with the entryway frescoes presenting the feats of the Roman hero Marcus Furius Camillus made in 1774 by Mariano de' Rossi, followed by the Galleria dei

Dodici Imperatori, entirely covered with precious marbles (Siena yellow, Sicilian jasper, cipolin) and decorated with porphyry busts of the Roman emperors.

The loggia with Giovanni Lanfranco's ceiling fresco was the only part of the seventeenth-century decoration that Marcantonio Borghese preserved. But it too was changed into a closed room and was completed with new frescoes by Domenico Corvi (1721–1803) in the lunettes. The villa was completely reworked, with contributions

from Gavin Hamilton, Felice Giani, Marchetti, Christoph Unterberger, De Maron, De Angelis, and Vincenzo Pacetti. Even the furnishings were changed, the leather removed from the walls and the peperino stone of the fireplaces replaced with boldly veined marble.

When Marcantonio died, the villa was inherited by Camillo Borghese, husband of Pauline Bonaparte, and in 1807, after applying much pressure, Napoleon succeeded in convincing his new brother-in-law to sell

OPPOSITE: The magnificence of the palace's entry hall is increased immeasurably by its splendid decoration, including many antique statues. The mosaic at the center of the floor was found during excavations in the properties of Terranuova; it presents a hunting scene and battles among wild animals and gladiators. The ceiling frescoes by Mariano Rossi present scenes from the life of Marcus Furius Camillus, and the late eighteenth-century decoration is by Vincenzo Pacetti, Francesco Corradori, Giovanni Monti, and Tommaso Righi.

the marble pieces decorating the villa. In all, 523 pieces left for France, including the *Borghese Gladiator,* the colossal heads of Antinous, Marc Aurelius, and Lucio Vero, and the *Hermaphrodite.* Fortunately, the statues that Scipione had commissioned from Bernini were thought to be of less interest, as was the collection of paintings, including the *Sacred and Profane Love* by Titian, bought by the cardinal himself. In 1827, Francesco Borghese bought the *Danae* by Correggio in Paris. In 1834 he extended the deed of trust to the works of art, saving many from dispersion. The Villa Borghese was acquired by the Italian state in 1902, after lengthy negotiations, and its museum still holds several works from the extraordinary art collection amassed by Scipione.

When Flaubert visited these halls with their striking opulence and beauty he claimed to see nothing but the statue of Pauline, to which he returned again and again, finally giving in to his emotion and kissing one of its smooth marble arms. Pauline Bonaparte herself was known for her passion, and it has been said that she was as intent on conquering men as was her brother Napoleon, just in a more intimate fashion. Asked how she could pose in the nude for the famous statue, she had replied merely, "There was a fire in the studio."

BELOW: The Hallway of the Emperors is named for the porphyry and alabaster portrait busts of the Roman emperors on display. The decoration above the doorway is the work of the sculptor Agostino Penna.

OPPOSITE: *Youth with Fruit Basket,* a masterpiece of the young Caravaggio, was one of the canvases confiscated from Cavaliere d'Arpino by Scipione Borghese, nephew of Paul V Borghese, in his insatiable desire to amass his collection of art and antiquities.

Casino Boncompagni Ludovisi

During the opening years of the seventeenth century many of the large agricultural holdings alongside Rome's Aurelian walls were transformed into villas and parks. The Villa Colonna, Villa Borghese, and Villa Ludovisi came into being over a short period of time, forming a kind of green belt marking off the dividing line between the great *Urbs* and the rolling fields of the countryside. Ludovico Ludovisi chose the ancient area of the gardens of Sallust as the site for what he intended to be Rome's most spectacular villa, a place where he might lead a life of leisure while glorifying his family. The measure of his success can be taken from the fact that two centuries later Stendhal wrote that "Nothing is more striking than these gardens lined with buildings, of which the Tuilleries and Versailles are but pale imitations."

Alessandro Ludovisi, Ludovico's uncle, was elected pope as Gregory XV (1621–23). He built his home "in only thirty months and surrounded it with pleasing pathways," as a chronicler reported. Elderly and in poor health, the pope was closely assisted by his enterprising nephew, who

The casino, part of the large villa that Ludovico Ludovisi had built when his uncle became Pope Gregory XV, takes its name from the fresco of Aurora by Guercino, made in 1621. In the lunette to the side of that painting is Night, mother of sleep and death, illuminated by reflected moonlight, testimony of the painter's interest in luministic effects; and Day, or Lucifer, bearing a torch.

can be said to have acted on his behalf as well as on his own. Although able to exploit the privileges of his uncle's position for no more than two years, he succeeded in making himself proprietor of extensive properties and in assembling one of the most striking collections of archaeological relics in the city. Cardinal Ludovico extended his property to take in the land and buildings of the Capponi and Del Nero families, eventually extending it over an area of thirty acres. These grounds were studded with orchards and vineyards, small woods and age-old trees and tall boxwood hedges. Five lesser buildings, designed to offer visitors places to rest, were located in the garden, along with fountains and ancient statues. The great obelisk that Pope Clement XII later moved to the Lateran Basilica once stood amid these Italian boxwood plants. Domenichino was brought in and instructed to design a labyrinth within a forest in which ancient statues could be hidden.

All that remains today of this extraordinary, boundless villa is one of the lesser buildings, the Casino dell'Aurora. It stands on land that belonged to Cecchino Del Nero and then to the celebrated Cardinal Del Monte before passing to the Ludovisi. It was probably designed by Maderno, creator of the Piombino Palace. It is cruciform, composed of a main central room giving on to four smaller rooms joined on the upper floor by a circular stairway. On top of the building is a lookout tower. The only reminder of the first owner is the inscription FRANCISCUS NERO SECRETARIUS APOSTOLICUS.

The Bologna-born artist known as Guercino (1591–1666) began working on the decoration in July 1621, shortly after his arrival in Rome, accompanied by Agostino Tassi, master of perspective architecture, who marked off the spaces of the vault. With his accumulated wealth, Cardinal Ludovico Ludovisi performed the role of patron of the arts with splendid results, offering particular support to Emilian artists, in keeping with the advice offered him by the learned Monsignor Agucchi. According to Giovanni Battista Passeri, a painter and author of a *Vite* ("Lives") that is a sequel to that by Baglione, the subject for the decorations was discussed by the erudite circle around the Marquis Bentivoglio, representative of the Este court in Rome. As is clear, the subject chosen was the glorification of the Ludovisi family by way of heraldic emblems, in that sense following the style used by the Farnese family in their villa at Caprarola. Early in the papacy of Gregory XV, the themes of Fame and Glory along with that of *Pontifex Maximus* were inaugurated, anticipating the themes narrated by Pietro da Cortona in Palazzo Barberini.

Guercino knew he had to do something to respond to Guido Reni in order to offer his contemporaries a passionate pictorial comparison to the vault of the *Aurora*, which Reni had painted in the casino of Scipione Borghese. He responded to Reni's classical, solemn harmonies with a rush of intimate and romantic feeling. The chariot of Aurora stands out against the sky in the center of the vault while the side lunettes present Day on one side and Night on the other. Two views of landscape, one of which shows the villa itself, flank the *quadratura* perspective views by Tassi. The representation of Night, illuminated by reflections of moonlight, is reminiscent of Venetian painting and testifies to the painter's interest in luministic effects. Presented with striking baroque foreshortening, Aurora is garbed in the glowing shades recommended in Cesare Ripa's manual of *Iconology*, newly published in 1618. Had the artist followed Ripa's dictates, the image would have been presented in orange, red, and white, with the arms and legs left naked. In many details, Guercino did follow Ripa's indications, spreading flowers all around and showing respect for emblems. It was certainly on his own initiative, however, that he had the chariot drawn by two dappled horses. Day, or Lucifer (in the sense of "light-bearing"), holds a torch in his hand, while Night, mother of sleep and death, suggests an image of romantic melancholy.

The decorations of the

side room involved contributions from four artists, who began work in 1621, each entrusted with creation of a landscape view while Tassi filled in the perspective frameworks around his dancing putti. The artists—Paul Bril, Giovan Battista Viola, Domenichino, and Guercino—worked side by side in a sort of tacit competition. Guercino, the youngest, presented beautiful damsels amid splashing fountains, providing a joyous interpretation of the works of Tasso. Paul Bril, a pioneer landscapist, mixed fronds and ruins, the entire scene covered with figurines. The learned Domenichino conceived a classical landscape with an elegiac tone; taken under the cardinal's wing and offered further protection by that theoretician of classicism Monsignor Agucchi, Domenichino became the Ludovisi family's favorite artist. The painting by Giovanni Battista Viola, *Landscape with Travelers*, is one of the only documented works by that Bolognese artist. It presents a romantic view with a Nordic flavor, daringly set on lonely mountain peaks.

Guercino also decorated the vault of the upper floor, which is the same size as the one below. The subject treated here is Fame. Spiral columns frame the ethereal presentation, which stands out against a shadowless sky. Honor and Virtue, dressed, respectively, in yellow and red, recall the heraldic motif of the Ludovisi family, borne

to auspicious glory by the immortal phoenix. An extraordinary bed, studded with precious gems, was in this room. According to Pinaroli (1725), it was supported by four columns of amethyst and lapis lazuli and encrusted with topazes, aquamarines, emeralds, and rubies. The headboard, decorated with ten large pearls, presented the chariot of Apollo, and the baseboard was made of carved agate and alabaster.

The ceiling of Cardinal

Del Monte's alchemical laboratory, part of the casino, had been decorated in 1597 by Caravaggio, who created allusions to the process of the transformation of base elements by presenting Jupiter, Neptune, and Pluto busy performing material transformations. In the middle, he painted the Cosmos, with the Earth still at the center of the universe as it was conceived before the scandalous revelations of Galileo. Water and Air are presented as

BELOW: The vault of the entranceway was frescoed in the mid-sixteenth century with grotesques. At the center is the head of Janus, emblem of the four seasons.

OPPOSITE: In 1621, Paul Bril, Giovanni Battista Viola, Domenichino, and Guercino were entrusted with creation of a "slice" of landscape to be inserted within perspective architecture by Agostino Tassi.

PAGE 300-301: Guercino, *Il carro dell'Aurora*, 1621.

changeable elements, capable of being transformed into solid or gaseous states. This is the only work Caravaggio is known to have made in oils on a wall. Corrupt and sophisticated, Cardinal Del Monte was Caravaggio's first patron, and he commissioned many canvases from him. The cardinal loved discovering young talents and had a great influence on his protégé, who lived in his palace near Piazza Navona as a paid retainer for five years, learning about the cardinal's eclectic interests, particularly experimental music and the natural sciences.

Prince Antonio Boncompagni Ludovisi added to the building in 1785, in particu-lar extending the two side wings. He did nothing, however, to alter the splendor of the decorations that Cardinal Ludovico had commissioned from the leading artists of his period. Nearby, to the side of the monumental entrance to the villa, was the Casino Capponi, which housed the cardinal's celebrated archaeo-logical collection until it was acquired by the Italian state early in this century to form the basis of the Museo Nazionale Romano.

ABOVE: On the first floor of the casino, Guercino painted *Fame, Honor, and Virtue*, dressed in yellow and red, the family's heraldic colors. Spiral columns frame the area of the presentation, which stands out against a cloudless sky.

OPPOSITE: The alchemical laboratory of Cardinal Del Monte (who had acquired the casino from the Del Nero family before it passed to the Ludovisi) was decorated in 1597 by Caravaggio, who alluded to the process of transmutation of elements by presenting Jupiter, Neptune, and Pluto busy performing material transformations; in the middle of the sphere is the Cosmos. This is the only work by Caravaggio done in oils on a wall.

Villa Albani

When, on the evening of November 20, 1700, the eminent Cardinal Giovanni Francesco Albani, a fervently religious man as well as a great patron of the arts, found himself proposed for the papal seat, he at first refused. He finally gave in to the will of the conclave and accepted the election but only with great reluctance and after much reflection. A series of edifying engravings by his protégé Pier Leone Ghezzi present scenes from his life as Pope Clement XI (1700–21): seeing to his religious duties with great diligence, giving communion, visiting the sick, humbly waiting on pilgrims at table. At the very same time, his nephew Alessandro Albani was dedicating an equal measure of zeal to collecting antiquities and forming a close circle of erudite lovers of things antique. Rome was then the capital city most loved by foreigners, who came there from every corner of Europe as part of the Grand Tour that every learned gentleman of the age felt himself nearly obliged to take. Painters and architects, sculptors and antiquarians, artists and men of letters of all sorts formed a

The villa was built by Carlo Marchionni between 1743 and 1763; its style shows the strong influence of the classical taste of its patron, Cardinal Alessandro Albani, an avid collector of antique works.

heterogeneous throng that poured into the city. These admirers of the past came to be dominated by the figure of the German classical archaeologist and historian Johann Joachim Winckelmann (1717–1778), who poetically exhorted others to love antiquity as the only true form of beauty. Cardinal Albani's treasures, destined to become one of the most extraordinary archaeological collections in the city, attracted a swarm of artists, led by the German painter of history paintings and portraits Anton Raphael Mengs (1728–1779), the Italian engraver and architect Giovanni Battista Piranesi (1720–1778), famous for his evocative versions of the past, and the Danish sculptor Albert Bertel

Thorvaldsen. These men, together with others of like spirit, were the leading exponents of what came to be known as the neoclassical movement. They considered the study of classical antiquity the supreme value in art and turned against baroque exuberance with the fervent rage of true revolutionaries. Winckelmann came to Rome in 1755, destined to spend most of the rest of his life in Italy. He and Mengs proved the most illustrious of those foreigners described by André Chastel as "doctrinaire and eager to formulate the elevated principles of culture." They were also inevitably destined to meet the enlightened cardinal.

In fact, the driving force behind this classical revival

came to be the exquisitely refined Villa Albani, a building that existed in the mind of the learned cardinal long before its first stone was set in place. On January 12, 1760, Vasi wrote that "the design of the villa and the lodge was conceived by His Eminence himself, but the decorations are the work of Carlo Marchionni, who has directed the construction, as can be seen in a portion of the wonderful garden." When still very young, the cardinal had founded an antiquarian academy to promote and study archaeological excavations. Around 1750, he asked the architect Carlo Marchionni to build a home for the collection he was assembling, the majority of which was later acquired by

The precious collection, in spite of the loss of 294 works taken to Paris by Napoleon, remains of extraordinary importance.

Clement XII for the Capitoline Museum. Today it is closed behind high gates, and we can only imagine what it was like when the Roman countryside spread out behind it all the way to the horizon, visible from the villa's double towers overlooking the city. On the facade of the building, a large arch with nine bays reminiscent of Palladio opens on the park, with the semicircular portico of the small building known as the coffee house in the background. A picturesque cornice supports the balustrade, which is lined with statues. Although much of the orderly hedges in the garden are today in poor condition, they still reveal Winckelmann's original intention of creating a mystical marriage of nature and the classical. Antique columns in porphyry, serpentine, granite, and oriental alabaster created a forest of colored stone. Walking through this open-air museum the cardinal and his guests encountered statues cleverly placed among the hedges. Winckelmann, then serving as the cardinal's secretary and adviser, came up with an overall decorative scheme based on his obsessive quest for harmony. Nor was anything left to chance in the room beneath the great ceiling fresco of Parnassus, made in 1761 by Mengs, whom Winckelmann called "The greatest artist of his time and perhaps also of later times, reborn like the phoenix from the ashes of

The interior of the villa bursts with opulent decoration created by such artists as Bicchierai, Clérisseau, La Piccola, Thorvaldsen, Anesi, and Mengs, all of them engaged to work in the classical style under the guidance of Winckelmann. In the Sala Ovata, which is topped by a dome, is a fresco by Bicchierai, showing Aurora, while at center sits Apollo, carved in Greek marble. In the ornate gallery, La Piccola made the grisaille works with cameos of antique subjects. Roman reliefs are set along the walls; the one over the doorway is of Antonio Pio.

Raphael to teach the world the beauty of art."

Other artists made contributions. Bicchierai, Charles-Louis Clérisseau, Nicolò La Piccola, Albert Bertel Thorvaldsen, Paolo Anesi, and Mengs succumbed to the will to create "Greek beauty" and took their inspiration from the classical models they had within reach, guided along the way by Winckelmann, considered today the father of modern scientific archae-ology and the first great historian of ancient art. The *Parnassus* was set between two perspective oculi, also painted by Mengs, showing *Love and Virtue*, *The Genius of the Arts*, and *The Glory and the Prize*. La Piccola made the grisaille work, with its cameos of antique subjects. Anesi painted landscapes with illusionistic openings toward the outdoors. Bicchierai had already finished the *Allegories of the Planets* in a baroque style that had been outdone by new artists. The prevalent aim was the narration of elevated, moralistic subjects with the sacrifice of rococo frivolities.

In a letter to the Danish sculptor and writer Johannes Wiedewelt in Copenhagen, dated August 18, 1759, Winckelmann recalls his familiarity with the cardinal, whose bed he used to sit on every morning for a little chat. He then had rooms in the palace on Via Quattro Novembre that he had re-stored (known today by the

ABOVE AND OPPOSITE: One room is named for a relief of Antinous, dating to the period of Hadrian, which is set above an elaborate fireplace. In that room, Paolo Anesi painted landscapes with illusionistic openings to the exterior. In a room to the side, Bicchierai made allegories of the planets in a late, somewhat outdated baroque style, while Anton Raphael Mengs fres-coed the celebrated vault with Parnasus (1756). A collection of ancient paintings is displayed in the side rooms.

name of the Del Drago family), and in the afternoons he accompanied the cardinal to the villa, "which was far more beautiful than the things that are made today, even when paid for by sovereigns." That version of antiquity related by Plutarch, that golden age of humanity, seemed to take on material existence in the reality of this wonderful structure.

Designed from its very conception as a setting for his archaeological collection, the cardinal never lived in this villa, then located outside the gates of Rome. Indeed, it never became a home and was always a private museum; as such, of course, it served as the forge for the birth of the neoclassical style. The villa's current owner, Prince Alessandro Torlonia, has decided to respect the cardinal's original intentions and does not live in the villa (which still has no electric lighting). Aside from the famous collection of antiquities, it holds many paintings of outstanding value, including a triptych by Nicolò da Foligno, known as L'Alunno, a sketch of the *Transfiguration* by Raphael, and works by Perugino and Luca Signorelli. Andrea Sperelli, the decadent hero of Gabriele d'Annunzio's novels, dreamed of possessing "a villa like that of Alessandro Albani, where the thick boxwoods, red oriental granite, white Luni marble, Greek statues, paintings from the Renaissance, and the very memories of the place

itself would compose the enchanting setting for some superb love affair."

BELOW: The attic relief on the walls from the golden age illustrates *The Punishment of Linceo*.

OPPOSITE: The vault of this elegant study is supported by fluted Corinthian pilaster strips; it is entirely decorated with ancient relics, including an Andromeda; the floor is composed of three excavated mosaics set in polychrome marble.

Selected bibliography

Affreschi del Cavalier d'Arpino in Campidoglio: analisi di un opera attraverso il restauro, Rome, 1980.

Amayden, T., *Storia delle famiglie romane*, Rome, no date.

Ammannato, C., *Via Giulia*, Rome, 1989.

Ashby, T., "The Palazzo Odescalchi in Rome," *Papers of the British School of Rome*, VIII, 1916 and 1920.

——. "The Capitol: Its History and Development," *The town planning review*, XII, 1927.

——. "The Palazzo Odescalchi in Rome," *Papers of the British School of Rome*, VIII, 1916.

Assunto, R., "Winckelmann a Villa Albani," *Committenza della famiglia Albani*, Rome, 1985.

Belli Barsali, I., *Ville di Roma*, Milan, 1970.

Borsi, F., *Palazzo Rondinini*, Rome, 1983.

Borsi, F., *Palazzo del Quirinale*, Rome, 1991.

Benzi, F., *Sisto IV Renovator Urbis. Architettura a Roma 1471–1484*, Rome, 1990.

Briganti, G., *Palazzo del Quirinale*, Rome, 1962.

Bruschi, A., *Bramante architetto*, Bari, 1969.

Càllari, L., *Le ville di Roma*, Rome, 1934.

——. *I palazzi di Roma*, Rome, 1944.

Cannatà, R., *Guida a Palazzo Spada*, Rome, 1984.

Carandente, G., *Il Palazzo Doria Pamphili*, Milan, 1975.

Chastel, A. and Morel, P., *La villa Médicis. Academie de France à Rome*, Rome, 1989.

Coarelli, F., *Guida archeologica di Roma*, Milan, 1974.

Coffin, D.R., *The Villa in the Life of Renaissance Rome*, Princeton, 1979.

——. *Gardens and Gardening in Papal Rome*, Princeton, 1991.

Colasanti, A., *Case e Palazzi barocchi di Roma*, Milan, 1912.

"Committenze della famiglia Albani," *Studi del Settecento romano*, Rome, 1985–1986.

Debenedetti, E., *Taccuini per la Villa Albani*, Rome, 1993.

De Feo, V., *La piazza del Quirinale. Storia, architettura e urbnistica*, Rome, 1973.

Della Pergola, P., *Villa Borghese*, Rome, 1962.

Errico, M.; Finozzi, S.S. and Giglio, I., "Ricognizione e schedatura delle facciate affrescate e graffite a Roma nei secoli XV e XVI," *Bollettino d'Arte*, 33–34, 1985.

Fagiolo Dell'Arco, M., *Bernini*, Rome, 1967.

Ferrerio, P., *Palazzi di Roma de' più celebri architetti*, Rome, 1650.

Forschungen zur Villa Albani, Berlin, 1989.

Frommel, C.L., *Baldassare Peruzzi als maler und Zeichner*, Vienna, 1967–68.

——. *Der römische Palastbau der Hocherenaissance*, I, Tubingen, 1973.

——. *Baldassarre Peruzzi. Pittura, scena e architettura nel Cinquecento*, Rome, 1987

——. *Raffael. Das architektonische Werk*, Stuttgart, 1987.

——. "La Villa Madama e la tipologia della villa romana nel Rinascimento," *Bollettino del Centro Internazionale di Studi di Architettura Andrea Palladio*, 11, 1969 (1970).

——. "Francesco del Borgo: Architekt Pius II und Paulus II. Palazzo Venezia, Palazzetto Venezia und San Marco," *Römisches Jahrbuch für Kunstgeschichte*, 21, 1984.

——. "Il Palazzo della Cancelleria," *Il palazzo dal Rinascimento a oggi*, conference proceedings of Reggio Calabria 1988, Rome, 1989.

———. "La villa Médicis et la typologie de la villa italienne à la Renaissance," *La Villa Médicis*, Rome, 1991.

Gavallotti Cavallero, D., *I palazzi di Roma dal XIV al XX secolo*, Rome, 1989.

Gerstfeldt, O. von, *Römische Villen*, Leipzig, 1909.

Golzio, V., *Palazzi Romani dalla rinascita al neoclassico*, Bologne, 1971.

Gonzales Palacios, A., "La mobilia di palazzo Pallavicini," *Arte Illustrata*, IV, 1971.

Gregorovius, F., *Storia della città di Roma nel Medio Evo*, Rome, 1900.

Gross, H., *Roma nel Settecento*, Bari, 1990.

Haskell, F., *Mecenati e pittori. Studio sui rapporti tra arte e società italiana dell'età barocca*, Florence, 1966.

Hermanin, F., *La Farnesina*, Bergamo, 1927.

Hibbard, H., *Carlo Maderno and Roman Architecture*, London, 1964.

Il Campidoglio di Michelangelo, Milan, 1965.

Il Quirinale, Rome, 1974.

Jannoni Sebastianini, C., *Le piazze di Roma*, Rome, 1972.

Lais, G., *Il terzo centenario della morte di San Filippo Neri a Palazzo Massimo*, Rome, 1983.

Laureati, L. and Trezzani, L., *Patrimonio artistico del Quirinale*, Rome, 1993.

Lefevre, R., *Villa Madama*, Rome, 1973.

Le Palais Farnese, Rome, 1980–81.

"Les fresques neopompeiennes du palais Taverne," *Connaissance des Arts*, 177, 1966.

Lizzani, M., *Palazzo del Quirinale*, Rome, no date.

Lombardi, F., *Roma, palazzi, palazzetti e case (1200–1870)*, Rome, 1991.

Lotti, L., "Palazzo Pallavicini e i suoi proprietari," *Alma Roma*, XV, 74, 3/4.

Manilli, J., *Villa Borghese fuori Porta Pinciana*, Rome, 1650.

Matthiae, G., *Roma Barocca*, Novara, 1974.

Morcelli, S.A., *La Villa Albani descritta*, Rome, 1869.

Munoz, A. and Colini, A.M., *Campidoglio*, Rome, 1931.

Neppi, L., *Palazzo Spada*, Rome, 1975.

Oltre Raffaello, Rome, 1984.

Palazzo Rondinini, Rome, 1983.

Palazzo Ruspoli, Rome, 1992.

Pecchiai, P., *Palazzo Taverna a Monte Giordano*, Rome, 1963.

Pertica, D., *Villa Borghese*, Rome, 1990.

Portoghesi, P., *Roma barocca*, Rome, 1967.

———. *Roma nel Rinascimento*, Milan, no date.

Rendina, C., *I Papi: storie e segreti*, Rome, 1983.

Rosati, F., "Palazzo Altieri ieri e oggi," *Capitolium*, 49, 1974.

Salerno, L., *Palazzo Rondinini*, Rome, 1965.

Schiavo, A., *Michelangelo architetto*, Rome, 1949.

———. *Palazzo della Cancelleria*, Rome, 1964.

———. "I palazzi dei Massimo," *Palazzo Braschi e il suo ambiente*, Rome, 1967.

Spagnesi, G.F., *Giovanni Antonio de Rossi*, Rome, 1964.

Tafuri, M., *La via Giulia*, Rome, 1973.

Tiberia, V., *Giacomo Della Porta*, Rome, 1974.

Tomei, P., "Un elenco dei palazzi di Roma al tempo di Clemente VIII," *Palladio*, 1939.

———. *L'architettura a Roma nel Quattrocento*, Rome, 1942.

Tonelli, G., *Ville di Roma*, Rome, 1968.

Toselli, G., *Palazzi di Roma*, Milan, 1965.

Torselli, G., *La Galleria Doria Pamphili*, Rome, 1969.

Via del Corso, Rome, 1961.

Villa Borghese, Exhibition catalog, Rome, 1966.

Voss, H., *Die Malerei des Barock in Rom*, Berlin, 1924.

Wittkower, R., *Art and Architecture in Italy 1600–1750*, Harmondsworth, 1975.

Wurm, H., *Der Palazzo Massimo alle Colonne*, Berlin, 1965.

Zaccagnini, C., *Le ville di Roma. Dagli "horti" dell'antica Roma alle ville ottocentesche*, Rome, 1976.

Zarina, A. and Korab, B., *I tetti di Roma. Le terrazze, le altane, i belvedere*, Rome (1976).

Zeri, F., *La Galleria Pallavicini*, Florence, 1959.

———. "The Pallavicini Palace and the Gallery in Rome," *Connaisseur*, 549, 1955.

Zeri, F. and Mortari, L., *La Galleria Spada in Roma*, Rome, 1970.

Addresses
of the palazzi
and villas

Villa Albani
via Salaria, angolo via di Villa
Albani
Property of Prince Alessandro
Torlonia, closed to the public
p. 306

Palazzo Altieri
piazza del Gesù, 49
Property of the Altieri family
and of A.B.I., closed to the
public
p. 194

Villa Boncompagni Ludovisi
via Lombardia, 46
Property of Prince
Boncompagni Ludovisi, closed
to the public
p. 298

Villa Borghese
piazzale Museo Borghese
Open daily except Monday
p. 282

Palazzo della Cancelleria
piazza della Cancelleria, 3
Property of the Santa Sede
family, closed to the public
p. 32

Casino dell'Aurora
via XXIV maggio, 43
Open the first day of each
month, tel. 06-4744019
p. 174

Castel Sant'Angelo
lungotevere Castello
Open daily
p. 76

Palazzo Chigi Odescalchi
piazza Ss. Apostoli, 80–81
Property of Prince Odescalchi,
closed to the public
p. 180

Villa Chigi detta La Farnesina
via della Lungara, 230
Property of the Accademia dei
Lincei and headquarters of the
national press office, open daily
p. 240

Palazzo dei Conservatori
piazza del Campidoglio, 1
Houses the Capitoline Museum,
open daily except Monday
p. 100

Palazzo Doria Pamphili
via del Corso, 304
Property of Prince Doria
Pamphili; via del Collegio
Romano, 3; offers access to
the Galleria Doria Pamphili,
open daily
p. 208

Palazzo Farnese
piazza Farnese, 67
Residence of the French
ambassador, closed to
the public
p. 52

Villa Giulia
piazzale di Villa Giulia, 9
Houses the National Museum at
Villa Giulia, open daily
p. 260

Villa Madama
via di Villa Madama, 1
Property of the Italian state,
authorized visits only
p. 252

Palazzo Massimo alle Colonne
corso Vittorio Emanuele, 141
Property of Prince Massimo,
closed to the public
p. 42

Villa Medici
viale Trinità dei Monti
Houses the Académie de
France, open for exhibitions
p. 268

Palazzo Pallavicini Rospigliosi
via XXIV maggio, 43
Property of Prince Pallavicini
Rospigliosi and the Federazione
Italiana dei Consorzi Agrari,
closed to the public
p. 160

Palazzo Pecci Blunt
via dell'Ara Coeli, 3
Property of the count Pecci
Blunt, closed to the public
p. 124

Palazzo del Quirinale
piazza del Quirinale
Seat of the President of the
Republic, closed to the public
p. 146

Palazzo Rondinini
via del Corso, 518
Houses the Circolo degli
Scacchi, closed to the public
p. 218

Palazzo Ruspoli Rucellai
largo Goldoni, 56
Property of Prince Ruspoli and
the law firm Memmo, first floor
open for exhibitions
p. 136

Palazzo Sacchetti
via Giulia, 66
Property of the marchese
Sacchetti, closed to the public
p. 112

Palazzo Savelli Orsini
via Monte Savello, 30
A private property of SMOM,
closed to the public
p. 66

Palazzo Spada
piazza di Capo di Ferro, 13
Houses the Counsel of State;
the Galleria d'Arte di palazzo
Spada is open daily except
Monday
p. 88

**Palazzo Taverna Gabrielli
Orsini**
via Monte Giordano, 36
Property of the marchese
Gallarati Scotti, closed to
the public
p. 230

Index of names and places

The names of the palazzi and villas featured in this volume appear in capital letters.